HAPPY INSIDE OUT

YOUR GUIDE TO UNDERSTANDING AND HANDLING EMOTIONS AND MOODS

MEETU SEHGAL

Made with ♥ on the Notion Press Platform
www.notionpress.com

Contents

Contents

Acknowledgements

This book is a compilation of my insights and wisdom from my emotional healing journey as an empath and highly sensitive individual. I've been fortunate to receive guidance from various mentors and teachers who have imparted invaluable lessons about navigating emotions, fostering love, and embracing life's challenges. They taught me to embrace my feelings not as burdens but as stepping stones on a path of spiritual growth. They nudged me to seek the silver lining in even the darkest clouds, reminding me that the good within never truly extinguishes.

My deepest gratitude goes to my parents, anchors of unwavering support, who instilled in me the belief that kindness forms the bedrock of any life well-lived; My mother, who taught me that it's necessary to be a good person before being anything else; my father, a karma yogi, who encouraged me to find my happiness in karma, always do my best and leave the results to the divine.

And to my friends, companions through sunshine and storm, I offer my heartfelt thanks. With you, I've shared the depths of meaningful conversations and found encouragement to keep going even when life presents its challenges.

Finally, I must acknowledge the profound learning journey that is my work as a therapist and coach. Each client entrusts me with their healing journey, and in working with them, I learn, I grow, I evolve.

This book is dedicated to all those who navigate life's highs and lows with intensity and sensitivity. It is my hope that the insights shared within these pages will serve as a guiding light for anyone seeking to embrace their emotions, cultivate resilience, and find meaning in everyday life.

Welcome, fellow travellers, to a journey unlike any other. Let's explore the tapestry of emotions together, thread by vibrant thread.

Preface

A Moody Story

Have you ever had one of those days when nothing went right?

Coffee spill on the shirt in the morning, stuck in bad traffic, a long queue at the bank and a warning disapproving look from the boss for being late can put anyone in a bad mood. What's happening underneath this bad mood is that each unfolding event elevates stress levels and puts your system on high alert, so you are geared up for the next unexpected twist.

All these emotions and the resultant lousy mood are entirely natural— simply a response to the environment. And that is what emotions are - a response to the immediate environment. When similar emotions are experienced in quick succession, they create a mood — positive or negative, depending on the nature of those emotions.

But if a mood is simply a response to our situations, why then do we demonise the so-called "negative emotions" and chase after happy or "positive emotions"? Why is feeling 'angry', 'sad', 'fearful', or 'envious' so bad when all these are just natural responses to the situations or events? Why do we dread bad moods and seek to always be in a good mood?

Let's imagine what would happen if no one ever felt a negative emotion or had a bad mood. Let us take the above example; if the person did not feel bad about being late and the boss giving them a disapproving look, they would never change their behaviour or think about the consequences of being late (one of which could be losing their job and financial security).

All beings (including humans) behave in ways that minimise pain and maximise pleasure; in other words, they increase rewards and avoid punishments. We tend to avoid behaviours that create pain or cause unpleasant situations. We always tend to gravitate towards rewarding activities, shy away from negative emotions and yearn for the comfort of positive moods.

But there are instances when we willingly engage in activities that involve discomfort but eventually bring us satisfaction and reward. Let's take bodybuilding and exercising as an example – initially, they cause pain, but the results are greatly rewarding. Similarly, learning something new can be mentally challenging, yet once we do it, we find satisfaction or some form of reward. As they say, No pain, no gain.

However, if some physical or intellectual discomfort is considered good (even rewarding), then why do we consider emotional pain so bad that we don't even acknowledge it or, worse, suppress it? Indeed, no one wants to feel the pain of negative emotions or be in a bad mood. But if it is a natural human phenomenon, is there a purpose to feeling all those emotions and bad moods?

Researchers have known for a long time now the biological processes behind emotions and moods. There are studies and research into the psychological aspects of mind and body, but sadly, most are from the disease perspective. It is only very recently that they have begun to study them from a health perspective rather than disease.

Due to a lack of information, negative emotions like fear, anger, shame, grief or guilt have often been misunderstood and associated with a psychological disorder instead of a healthy human response. Because of this, negative emotions are not even discussed in a constructive manner, and no one knows what to do about it. At best, one is advised not to pay attention to it; at worst, one is labelled with a behavioural problem or mental disorder.

Even if anyone talks about them, the focus is on control. But the truth is, you can't handle (let alone control) something that you don't fully understand.

Another issue with this is that in this modern, fast-paced world, we don't have the time to process what we feel. We keep carrying the burden of those emotions and moods but never come down to addressing them until one day, they just explode from within in the form of panic attacks, depression or other forms of mood disorders.

And no one teaches us how to manage what we feel either. As a result, when we feel uncomfortable or any "negative" emotion, we look for an escape, scared like a caveman running away from lightning or any unfamiliar threat.

This book is an effort to initiate a discussion on emotions, feelings, and moods and offer guidance on understanding and managing them in simple and healthy ways for you and those around you.

Occasionally, I will discuss certain scientific and biological aspects to provide insights and reasons behind why we feel what we feel. Knowledge is power. The more you understand something, the better you are equipped to deal with it.

The ultimate goal of this book is to normalise emotions and moods, overcome any resistance towards the so-called "negative" emotions and states, and develop healthy coping mechanisms, both from a lifestyle and spiritual perspective.

The book is divided into two parts; the first part is about understanding emotions, moods and energy. You will explore emotions from different perspectives — biologically, energetically and spiritually. You will learn about moods and emotions, how they come to be, and their role in our lives.

The book's second part is dedicated to ways and techniques for handling emotions and moods. This part is further subdivided into two. In the first part, you will explore ways and techniques that you can do physically to work with emotions and moods. The second part is more spiritual, where you will find energy techniques, psychological tools, and spiritual ways of dealing with emotional journeys. You can choose to use one or more than one method in combination that best works for you.

My invitation to you is to try different combinations and tools, develop an open attitude to dealing with the energy of emotions and understand that emotions are not a weakness; when you feel, it means you are still alive. This book is for you if you feel too much or too little or are afraid of all the dormant feelings within you and would like to know what to do with them.

Disclaimer: This book is about emotions, but it's not a doctor. If you are facing any mental health challenges, please reach out to a trained doctor or professional. They can provide personalised guidance and support based on your individual needs and circumstances. The information presented in this book is intended for educational and informational purposes only and should not be construed as medical advice. It is not a substitute for professional medical diagnosis or treatment. Don't try to heal yourself with just this book, and remember, everyone's different.

Stay safe!

It is important to remember that everyone experiences emotions differently. What works for one person may not work for another. Always listen to your own body and intuition when making decisions about your emotional well-being.

Part I

Understanding Moods and Emotions

CHAPTER ONE

Mood and Emotions

"We work with nutrition and exercise to increase our energy, but we ignore the richest source of energy we possess—our emotions."

— Karla McLaren, The Language of Emotions: What Your Feelings Are Trying to Tell You

It's mind-boggling how little is known about emotions and feelings by the larger population that is not made up of researchers and scientists.

It is even sad that talking about emotions or feelings is considered a sign of weakness. If this is weakness, then feeling hungry is a sign of weakness too, because emotions and moods are a completely natural phenomenon.

Emotions are either dismissed as annoying or insignificant or brushed under the rug and suppressed in our day-to-day lives. But we don't realise the power they hold over us from under that rug too.

Emotions are what make us more human, capable of feeling happiness, sadness or joy. Without them, we would be nothing more than robots.

Mood is another term we use so often, but we do not even stop to think about it. It is so deeply a part of our vocabulary and life in general. How many times have you used statements like these:

What are you in the mood for?

Put on some music to set the mood.

He's moody today; I think you should wait to ask this.

The good news lifted her mood.

I am in a good mood today.

Some examples of mood are humorous, romantic, mysterious, light-hearted. Mood is such a common word with many associations in our minds that we don't even stop to consider what it really is, why we are feeling it, and what we can do about it.

Understanding and addressing emotions and moods is vital because they affect how we perceive and respond to the world around us.

For example, if you are in a bad mood or experiencing a negative emotion and then your significant other does something to annoy you, all the bad things about your relationship with them will surface. In such a state, it will be challenging for you to listen and empathise with your partner and sort out the problems with them. Similarly, when you are in love, you feel elated and joyful and are in a good mood. The world seems to appear very beautiful, and not many things can bother you at that time. It will be easy for you to forgive your partner for any insignificant thing.

Moods and Emotions move in Cycles

People often avoid negative emotions and moods and always want to be happy. But moods and emotions are a part of being human, and just as life moves in a cycle, moods, too, have a rhythm.

Life moves in a cycle; there are happier times and times of struggle and sadness. Combined, they make the cycle complete, just like day and night. Without one, the other cannot exist.

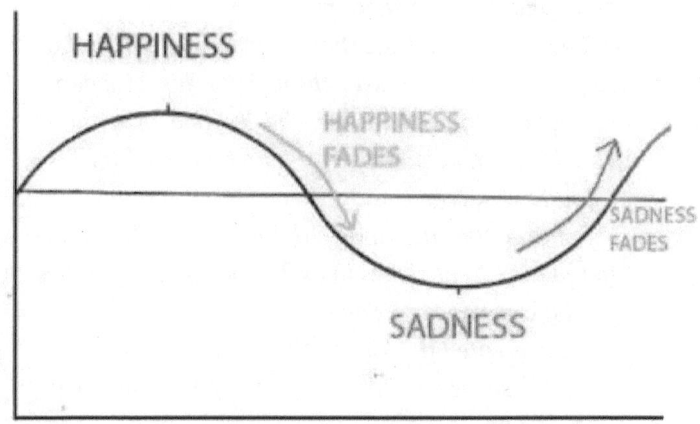

Cycle of Emotions

It is when the rhythm breaks and a mood or emotion persists for a more extended period that is when it is necessary to do something about it - whether it's through natural methods of mood regulation or medicines from a doctor.

Indian spirituality talks about non-attachment. This non-attachment does not mean being cold-hearted. It means you are not attached to the happiness in the up-cycle, nor are you afraid of the sadness in the down-cycle.

You welcome both as part of life. Whatever happens, if you can remind yourself that "This too shall pass", that is when you can experience the bliss of existence.

This too shall pass

The saying "this too shall pass" has origins attributed to Persian Sufi poets such as Rumi, Sanai, and Attar of Nishapur.

The story goes that there was once a king who sought wisdom tirelessly throughout his kingdom but found none. Eventually, he learned of a man living in a remote part of his realm renowned for his profound wisdom.

Summoning the man to his court, the king offered him great riches in exchange for sharing the secret of his wisdom. The man agreed.

He presented the king with a small box, much to the king's surprise and disappointment. Inside was a simple ring.

Disgruntled, the king asked, "Is this all?"

The wise man calmly replied, "Place the ring on your finger and read the inscription aloud."

The king complied, reading the words engraved on the ring: "This too will pass."

The wise man then explained, "Wear this ring always and look upon it regularly. Whether in times of joy or hardship, remember that everything is transient, and this too shall pass.""

Just as no situation is permanent, so are the emotions and moods. If you just notice and stay with what you feel, the feeling will pass within a few minutes.

But in life, we experience that certain emotions and moods do not pass easily or quickly. They take time and effort and cause discomfort as you experience them.

Just as the body's muscles take time and practice to build, the muscle or skill of handling emotions too takes time, practice, persistence and desire to do it. As a therapist and coach, I often tell my clients, "You cannot practice on a battlefield. You need peace to practice". Use the tools mentioned in this book every day; they will help you deal with emotions on an everyday basis. And when the big bang of emotion happens, you will be ready and able to handle it well.

You cannot create peace, joy or harmony; that's the beauty of it because they already exist within us. They just get covered by the debris of everyday living.

Have you ever seen an abandoned house that hasn't been cleaned for decades? It is full of dust, grime and cobwebs. It looks hopeless. But as you begin to clean it, little by little, the house starts to reveal its beauty, its carved furniture, tiled walls and the exquisite mosaic floors. We are similar to that house which is cleaned from the outside every day, but the insides haven't been cleared for a long time. The techniques in this book will help you do the inner clearing to reveal the beauty - the peace, joy and harmony within.

CHAPTER TWO

What are Emotions?

"Without our emotions, we can't make decisions; we can't decipher our dreams and visions; we can't set proper boundaries or behave skilfully in relationships; we can't identify our hopes or support the hopes of others; and we can't connect to, or even find, our dearest loves."

— Karla McLaren, The Language of Emotions: What Your Feelings Are Trying to Tell You

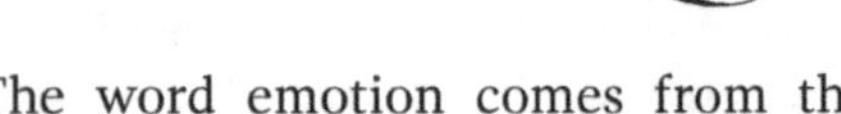

The word emotion comes from the Latin root emoter, which means "Energy in Motion" (E-motion). Emotions are a form of energy that comes up in response to situations. Their job is to help bring our awareness to the present and pay attention to something in the environment. They also provide us with the necessary energy to respond and take action as a result.

There are many emotions like happiness, anger, sadness, fear, disgust, shame, etc. Each one serves a purpose. Anger helps you restore boundaries; sadness enables you to let go of the past; fear helps you bring your attention to any threats; and disgust helps you discern food from poison and survive.

According to psychologists, there are six basic emotions - fear, disgust, anger, surprise, joy, and sadness. Each of these can be combined or mixed to form more types of emotions as shown in the wheel of emotions.

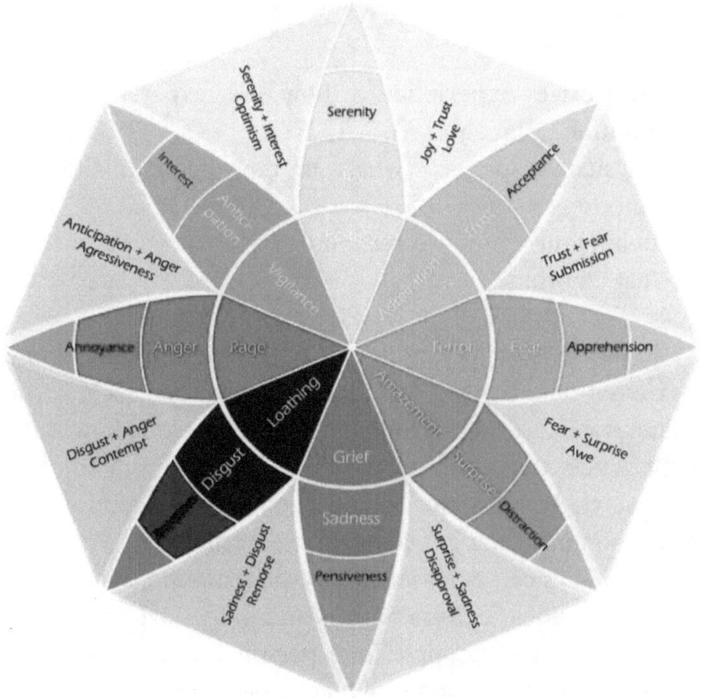

Wheel of Emotions by Plutchik

Emotions are a powerful force like water. When stored water is released from the dam, if not done properly, it can wreak havoc. Similarly, emotions can cause harm when suppressed for too long – they will either weaken the system and lead to health problems or burst forth uncontrollably, destroying relationships and mental health. If emotions are such a powerful force, imagine what can happen when you learn to use them better, when emotions become your allies.

According to Don and Sandra E. Hockenbury, emotions are complex psychological states that have three components:

1. **Subjective experience** - how we experience each emotion uniquely
2. **Physical response** - what our body feels in different emotions
3. **Behaviour** - how we respond to a situation because of that emotion

Emotion is energy, and it is felt in the body. Everyone has emotions; that's a fact. But not everyone feels it the same way. It differs from person to person, how they experience the emotion, where they feel it and how intensely[1]. For example, some people feel anger in their chest, some in their gut, some in their arms, etc.

The physical experience of the emotion is entirely subjective. Socio-cultural norms and individual upbringing influence it. For example, one person might break down during a financial crisis, while another might be more resilient.

Also, we don't always feel one emotion purely. We can experience a mix of emotions too. For example, starting a new job can make you feel excited and nervous. Having a child can bring both joy and anxiety and a whole range of other emotions.

The Problem with Emotions

It might seem somewhat difficult to imagine but emotions can be your friend and guide, even the more difficult ones. They can help you navigate situations and help you stay in touch with reality if you will listen to them. Emotions are like smoke detectors for humans. Their job is to help you survive through life-threatening situations.[2] Their primary function is to bring your attention to your environment.

Emotions become a problem in two situations:

1. They are not allowed to flow in a healthy manner but are suppressed or thrown out on others
2. They are triggered by the slightest of stimulus.

Let us talk about these two situations separately.

1. Not letting emotions flow

"Good girls don't get angry."

"Boys don't cry."

Remember hearing these statements?

Most of us are not taught what to do with what we feel; worse, we are taught the wrong messages. When we feel something, especially negative, we tend to run away from that emotion like a headless chicken, not knowing what to do with it. Some everyday things we do are, distract ourselves from feeling it, suppress it or try to express that energy through certain destructive behaviours.

For example, some people act out in anger using harsh words or actions. In contrast, others do it in a passive-aggressive manner through silent treatment and withdrawing love and attention. And then some are well-trained not to express their anger, so much so that they keep burying and suppressing those feelings until a volcano is ready to explode.

We all have different strategies to deal with various emotions which we learnt from our parents, caretakers, siblings and elders around us in our growing years. The above example shows different strategies/behaviours for anger, but we have strategies for everything - fear, sadness, guilt, happiness, joy, excitement, disgust, etc.

If you are fortunate, your parents or caretakers will have known how to handle and respond to emotions healthily and will have passed on that skill to you. But in most cases, that does not happen, and you end up learning behaviours or beliefs about emotions that are not healthy.

There are many beliefs around emotions and expressing them. Some of the common ones are:

1. Talking about emotions means you are weak and vulnerable.
2. Emotions should not be shared openly; otherwise, people can take advantage of you.
3. It is not polite or appropriate to express emotions openly (sometimes even considered obscene in many Asian cultures to express joy openly)
4. Men don't cry
5. Negative emotions are not ok (for example, you should not get angry, you should not worry, don't be sad etc.)

Such beliefs about emotions do not allow you to acknowledge them, feel them or let them flow. This leads to dysregulated emotions and the nervous system.

Emotions are like rivers that need to flow. A flowing river is healthy. But when emotions are not allowed to flow, they begin to collect inside like a swamp. If you have not allowed yourself to feel something, don't think it's over now. Chances are they are rotting inside, becoming stale, waiting to be expressed through other means.

If it was a one-off emotion, it might fizzle out. But if it is something you feel often and suppress it, not allowing it to flow, not letting yourself feel it, that energy keeps collecting inside, becoming poison. Gradually, it affects your mind (colouring your thoughts), relationships (both with others and self) and eventually your health.

Louise Hay talks in detail about how various emotions affect our mind and body in her book 'You Can Heal Your Life'. She reveals the connection between emotions, thought patterns and health problems.

> *"Dr Jill Bolte Taylor, author of 'My Stroke of Insight'talks about emotions as a 90-second process;*
>
> *"When a person has a reaction to something in their environment, there's a 90-second chemical process that happens; any remaining emotional response is just the person choosing to stay in that emotional loop.""*

When something happens in our environment, chemicals are flushed through our body to put it on alert mode. It takes less than 90 seconds to flush out those chemicals from the body. This is phenomenal because this means that, for 90 seconds, if you become totally present to your emotion, watch it come up, notice the associated feelings, and then watch it go away, the emotion has left your body.

If you feel anything after this, pay attention to the thoughts that are re-stimulating the reaction over and over again.

If you can be totally present for your emotions, you will notice that emotions bring the gifts of awareness, letting go, standing up for yourself and so many more. When you allow your emotions to flow, honour them for the gifts they bring and watch them leave; you no longer need to suppress them. In setting them free, you set yourself free.

Flow of Emotions from the perspective of Energy Meridians

We are energy beings. Life force energy flows through us and each cell and atom of our body is made up of energy. Simply put, the reason we are physical beings is because, scientifically, the waves of energy slowed down enough for us to become visible.

We are made up of energy and energy flows through us constantly. But it does not flow randomly. There are patterns to its flow and the flow happens through energy meridians. According to some Sanskrit texts, our body has 72,000 energy meridians, also known as nadis.

> "***Interesting fact:*** *The number of nadis or energy meridians varies according to different scriptures. According to Goraksha Samhita and Hatha Yoga Pradipika, the number of nadis is mentioned in the number 72000, while in Shiva Samhita the number of nadis is mentioned as 350,000. Out of thousands of nadis, 72 nadis are considered important. Out of these main nadis, the 3 most important ones are IDA, PINGALA and SUSHUMNA.*"

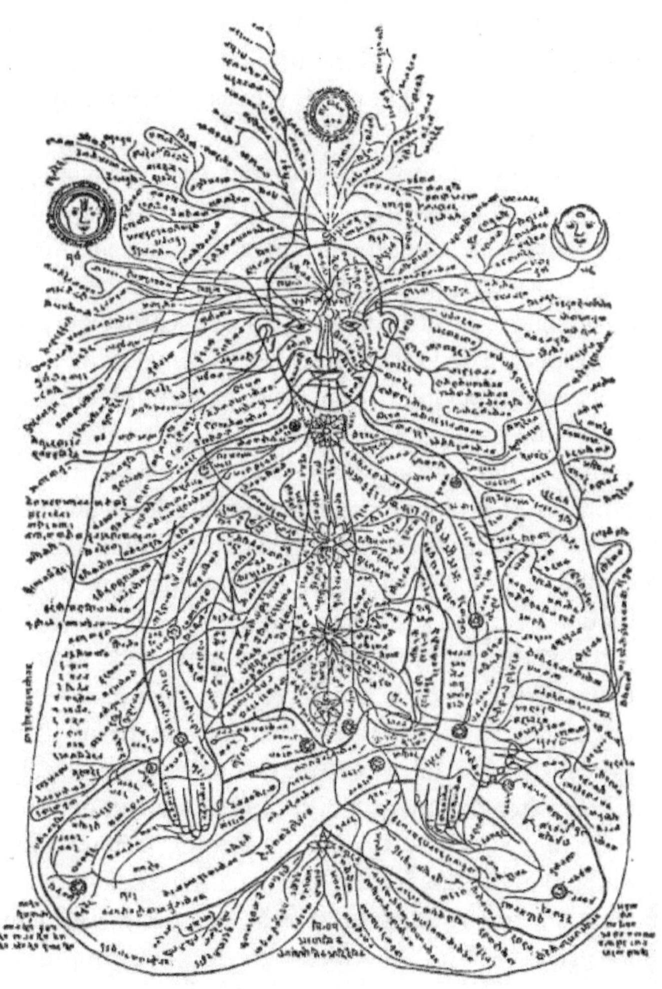

Energy Meridians in the Body

Consider energy meridians like highways with free-flowing traffic of energy. Since emotions are energy, they, too, flow through these meridians. Each emotion has a specific frequency and vibration. The so-called negative emotions are denser than positive ones, which means they move slower.

If slow-moving traffic got in the way of high-speed traffic, it would create traffic jams. That's what happens in energy meridians when the negative emotions are flowing through it without finding any way to get out. It begins to jam the energy through the meridians, eventually creating energy blocks. The longer these blocks remain, the denser they become, blocking energy flow through the meridians to organs and tissues.

Studies in energy medicine and alternative therapies have proven that any physical ailment begins as an energy block and gradually progresses towards becoming a disease, sometimes taking as long as six years. When the energy is blocked in meridians, the organs and tissues in the body do not receive the required energy to do the work, gradually reducing their efficiency and developing a disease.

Dr. David Hawkins, researcher and author of 'Power vs. Force', demonstrates emotions as energy. He devised a scale that rates the energy level of basic human emotions, with a range of 1 to 1,000. Anything below 200 is considered unhealthy for the individual and society (shame 20, guilt 30, apathy 50, grief 75, fear 100, desire 125, anger 150, pride 175). Anything above 200 represents constructive expressions of power (courage 200, neutrality 250, willingness 310, acceptance 350, reason 400, love 500, joy 540, peace 600, enlightenment 700 -1000).[25]

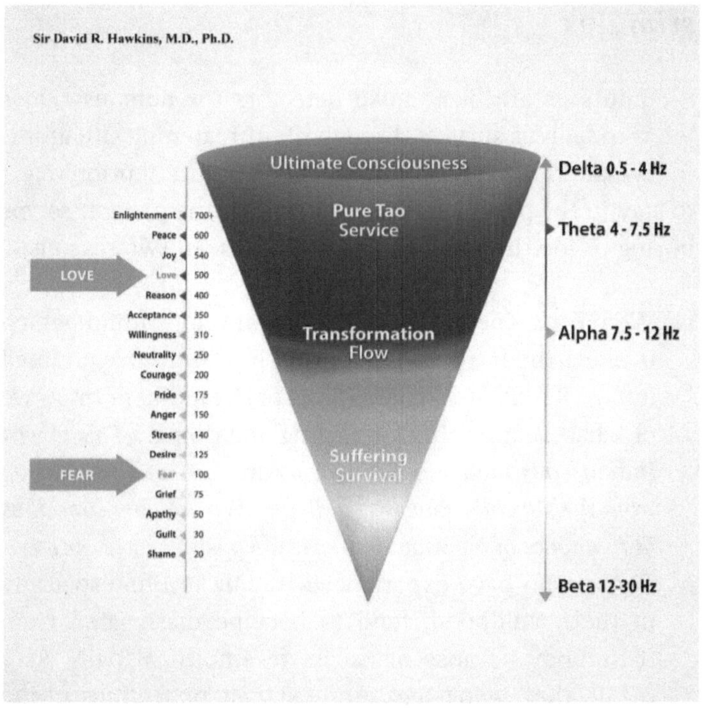

Energy of Emotions

The premise of energy healing systems is – to cure the energy block, the disease cures itself. It restores the body's own healing system by clearing the energy pathways and helping the body heal itself.

This shows that letting the emotions flow out of the system is essential to good health. There are plenty of healthy ways to do that mentioned in the second part of the book.

2. Emotions are triggered at the slightest stimulus

Emotions are like smoke detectors for humans. Their job is to help us survive through life-threatening situations.

We are rarely present in the NOW. Our attention tends to stay in the past or future, especially if the present seems boring or too threatening. This is because of two reasons:

1. We mostly operate from the subconscious mind, which is like a robot, replaying all that has been programmed into it. Rarely are we conscious of the moment or aware of what we are thinking, feeling and doing. (*This is why Indian spirituality focuses on awareness and waking up from the subconscious way of living. We are only conscious in moments of emotional intensity – positive or negative.*)
2. Those who have experienced trauma in life, especially in their childhood, tend to become dissociated from their body because of excessive emotional pain. As a result, they won't feel subtle signals or feelings in the body happening in the present.

In such situations, emotions play a very powerful role in helping us get back to this moment where things are happening, alert us to any potential threats and give us the required energy to act on this stimulus.

> *"Dissociation is a process in which a person disconnects from their thoughts, feelings, memories, behaviours and physical sensations. You essentially break contact between the body and the brain to survive the experience. Trauma-related dissociation is also known as mental escape. It*

happens because physical escape is no longer possible, or the person is so emotionally overwhelmed that they can no longer cope. This is almost like switching off.

Dissociation is one of the ways your brain protects you. It doesn't want you to relive your traumatic experience, so it freezes and dissociates that trauma. Dissociation can also happen when you encounter a situation that reminds your nervous system of the trauma (consciously or unconsciously).

But in doing so, you also become dissociated from the present moment. Dissociation doesn't erase the trauma. While it may offer temporary relief, the underlying issues still need to be addressed for true healing. Inner Child Healing helps you process and heal the trauma without re-traumatizing you, helping you integrate the parts frozen and dissociated. "

But if the smoke detectors become very sensitive, that is, emotions are triggered at the slightest of stimulus, this will mean that the emotions would be triggered even when there is no real need for them. There would be many false alarms triggering the nervous system into high alert and a flood of chemicals, emotions and sensations in the body when there is no real threat or situation. Many anxiety or panic attacks are because of false alarms and sensitive triggers.

This could happen when a person has had experiences (trauma in childhood or otherwise) that have given the mind the impression that it's not safe out there. Whether it's one traumatic experience (causing PTSD) or multiple experiences (creating complex PTSD), it rewires the brain to become hyper-vigilant to external threats. This leads to the slightest of things to trigger a barrage of emotions.

Trauma and its link to Emotional sensitivity

Enough has been written about stress, depression and anxiety. But not enough is known by the layperson about its roots which is the underlying trauma. Let's first demystify the word "trauma".

When people hear the word trauma, they think of the big traumatic events (big T) like sexual abuse, violence, a catastrophic life-changing event, etc. But not many understand that trauma can also be the smaller events that happen regularly (small t).

> "*Dr. Thema Bryant, author of the book "Homecoming: Overcome Fear and Trauma to Reclaim Your Whole, Authentic Self," says that trauma involves "life events and life circumstances that can make it very difficult for us to survive, for us to function, for us to relate to other people, for us to feel good about ourselves."* "

People recognise Big T traumatic events, but they often dismiss the small t events (because of lack of awareness) as "not too bad", "it was nothing", "it doesn't matter", etc. One needs to understand that trauma isn't just about what happened but also about how it affected you and how you responded to it. Any event or situation that causes distress, fear and a sense of helplessness is a small t trauma.

It's true that the Big T events leave a lasting impact on the psyche, but the small t events cause more problems with the basic blueprints of life.

Small t Trauma and Blueprints of Life

By blueprints, I refer to how we believe life and other aspects of it should be, our rules of life and everything in it, for example, relationships, career, money, health, etc. We only create/attract what's in our blueprint. There is very little chance that we will attract something that is not a part of our blueprint, our pattern, without doing the inner work.

A blueprint is formed when a child is observing life, the elders, parents, caretakers, teachers, and friends. According to Dr Bruce Lipton, up to the age of 7, the child is in a hypnotic state, which means they are a sponge absorbing everything they see, hear and experience[3]. At this stage, they cannot decipher if something is wrong or right; they are just taking in and learning everything about life. This creates blueprints in their mind about life. And this blueprint keeps getting created repeatedly until you consciously change it.

Good blueprints create happier circumstances, and not-so-good or unhealthy blueprints create problematic situations and relationships. Small t traumatic events that are recurring and often in early childhood impact the blueprints of the child. This leads to the symptoms of PTSD (Post Traumatic Stress Disorder), like hypervigilance, increased sensitivity, anxiety, dissociation, etc., becoming a part of the blueprint and seeming like the norm, as if they are a part of who you are.

This means that the abuse is also normalised in the blueprint of the child. When the child grows up, they will tend to attract relationships (personal and professional) that will replicate the abuse in varying degrees, thus keeping the person in the same cycle of traumatic events (which now have become part of everyday life) and keep creating and adding to the already existing anxiety, hyper-alertness, dissociation, anger issues, depression and so on.

Trauma alters emotional sensitivity

It is now clinically known that trauma physically alters different parts of the brain and neural connections.

When the part of the brain responsible for survival is activated repeatedly in early childhood, it changes the way the other parts of the brain connect with each other. As a result, the way a lot of cognitive functions work in the brain are altered. It affects the ability to learn, form memories, learn, think, reflect, respond to stimuli and regulate emotions. Therefore, it is not just that trauma affects the perspective; it also physically affects how the brain develops. The developing brain remembers the traumatic experiences, affecting the survival response, which can get triggered even when there is no real danger.[4]

Research has proven that childhood trauma is associated with medical conditions in adulthood, such as heart disease, stroke, cancer, chronic pain, and fibromyalgia. Major stress because of traumatic incidents can overload the nervous system, causing changes in the brain. It can lead to depression, anxiety, flashbacks and dissociation.

Your brain's primary purpose is to keep you safe and help you survive. Due to trauma (Big T and small t), the brain learns to perceive and respond to situations and events in a certain way, to maximise your chances of survival, thus altering how you will respond to future events that may be similar to the original event. In other words, it tweaks the smoke detectors to a more sensitive setting so that they go off more easily. This will ensure you respond to every alarm, maximising your chances of survival, but this will also lead to more false alarms.

> "*"Traumatized people chronically feel unsafe inside their bodies: The past is alive in the form of gnawing interior discomfort. Their bodies are constantly bombarded by visceral warning signs, and, in an attempt to control these processes, they often become expert at ignoring their gut feelings and in numbing awareness of what is played out inside. They learn to hide from their selves." (p.97)*
>
> *— Bessel A. van der Kolk, The Body Keeps the Score: Brain, Mind, and Body in the Healing of Trauma*"

This is one of the reasons some people are more sensitive to things and people around them. I am not including the Highly Sensitive Person (HSP) or empaths here. Their responses are due to their highly sensitive nervous systems and mirror neurons (which, in some cases, according to experts, could be a response to early childhood trauma[5]) that give them the ability or tendency to feel intensely.

If you find yourself becoming increasingly angry, having outbursts, or sad with crying spells and can't find any immediate reason for it, this could mean a past traumatic event that is unresolved is still affecting you. Until that event or series of events are not healed, the mind keeps reliving them as if they are happening in the present, thus creating the same chemicals of stress and the same feelings that you felt back then.

For the mind, there isn't much difference between imagination and reality. If it imagines something, it is real for it. If the mind remembers something and there is still an emotional charge to it, it will be real for the body.

Time does not heal; healing heals; time just buries it down, but its poisonous effect keeps leaking out, affecting your everyday life. This is why it's important to process what happened in a safe space with a professional so that what happened is no longer still happening in your mind; it becomes a chapter that you can move on from.

> “*“When society looks at someone struggling, they say: What's wrong with them? And when a trauma-informed person sees them, they say: What happened to them?”*
>
> *— Dr. Thema Bryant*”

In the second part of this book, we explore how to handle emotions better and how we can reset our sensitivity switches.

CHAPTER THREE

WHAT ARE MOODS?

"What happens when that recently triggered mood lingers? You've been in a bit of a funk since that day, and now you look around the room during a staff meeting and all you think of is that this person's tie is hideous, and the nasally tone of your boss is worse than nails on a chalkboard."

— Joe Dispenza

Oxford Dictionary describes Mood as "the way that you are feeling at a particular time".

Collins dictionary defines Mood as a temporary state of mind or temper.

Scientists define a mood as feelings over a prolonged period and thoughts that mirror those feelings. (Watson & Clark, 1997[6])

A study into understanding moods has led scientists to believe that moods are created by experiences happening close together in time. Moods are simply emotions that "spill over" from their respective events or situations. The event is over, yet the emotional responses of the event continue, thus creating a mood.

For example, reaching the office late and then losing a sale from a client is enough to put anyone in a bad mood.

When this spillover becomes prolonged and severe, so much so that there seems to be no reason for it, then it becomes a mood disorder.

Moods are generally defined as good or bad (positive or negative). For example, if you are in a bad mood, you might feel upset or stressed, and your thoughts will generally follow the pattern too. Similarly, when you are in a good mood, you might feel happy, joyful, loving, grateful, etc.; those emotions and moods will also colour your thoughts and perceptions about your environment.

Mood and Emotions

Moods are quite similar to emotions as they are so intricately linked. Yet there are some essential differences between the two. The key difference between mood and emotion is time and context.

Moods are generally long-lasting (hours-days), whereas emotions may last a few minutes.

Emotions tend to be about something specific, your most recent experiences with a person or situation. It is a direct result of what's happening in your immediate environment. Mood is generally caused by multiple events over a period of time, not necessarily the reaction to what is happening around you in the immediate present.

Moods are not as intense as emotions. At times, you may not even be aware of moods until you notice your response to situations.

Actions taken in certain moods can create conflict and chaos or harmony and love. Human beings, no matter how rational, are affected by experiences and emotions, which are the two main ingredients for creating moods. It is referred to as emotional thinking, a phenomenon where our feelings shape our thoughts.

We never see the world as it is; we always see it through lenses. These lenses (also known as filters or perspectives) are made of our beliefs about self and the world, cultural and social norms and our experiences. A major factor that colours these lenses is how we are feeling at this moment and what our mood is.

There is a popular saying, "Never make a decision when you are upset, angry or very happy". When in a good mood, everything feels easy and loving, but when one is in a bad mood, even the best experiences feel like there is something wrong or missing. This is why it's so important to understand and deal with our moods so that we don't become a puppet in their hands.

Why do we experience moods?

We hear a lot about rectifying and dealing with moods and mood swings; it gives us the impression that having moods is not right. But moods are not a result of something wrong with us. Moods are natural and essential.

Moods help us with survival[7]. It sounds counter-intuitive, but here is the truth.

Everything we do is determined by reward or punishment; or simply pain or pleasure. We will naturally tend towards activities that are rewarding and bring pleasure, and we will always make efforts to move away from things that bring us punishment or pain.

For example, one will, ideally, move away from behaviours that might mean losing the job and financial security but will move towards activities that will help them make more money and have financial security. Similarly, one will always move away from negative emotions because they cause pain and find ways to have more positive emotions and pleasure.

We always tend to anticipate (and predict to an extent) what will happen tomorrow (or in future). This tendency is hardwired from the times when humans were hunters and gatherers. The prediction of finding food and surviving tomorrow was dependent in a big way on today and specifically on two factors –

1. Today's experience of events and
2. Our physical state (ability to cope with it) today

If food was readily available today and the body is fit (not injured), it means tomorrow is likely to have similar results and survival is ensured; hence, the mood will be positive and uplifted. But if food was scarce today and an injury happened while hunting, it would lower the possibility of finding food tomorrow, reducing chances of survival. This would have dampened the mood because tomorrow's expectations for food and survival seemed bleak.

This change in mood did the work of setting expectations realistically and helping one to change tactics and behaviours accordingly. This is how moods have played a role in helping humans survive.

The purpose of the mood (good or bad) is to help us adapt our behaviour (and also manage our expectations) to the situations that might happen in the future. In today's scenario too, moods play a similar role, helping you predict tomorrow's outlook and setting the right expectations to influence necessary behavioural or strategy change. Moods also work as a buffer to protect you from unexpected situations and prepare you for them mentally.

How many times has it happened that events of today determined your mood for tomorrow or the next couple of days?

For example, if an athlete injured their foot today in a practice session, they may be unable to participate or perform well in their upcoming race. Suppose you hit a jackpot today or got promoted with a bonus. In that case, chances are you will be able to deal with any unexpected expenses that may come up in the near future.

If something good hasn't happened in a while, your expectation of a positive event lowers. But if something bad has been happening (even if it is no longer happening), it raises your expectations of something bad to happen. This is why trauma creates PTSD. It leaves an impact on the nervous system and prepares it to cope with the possibility of it happening again tomorrow.

You may ask, "Why are emotions not sufficient for this purpose?" Emotions are a response to one event and only last for minutes. Moods are a result of a series of events happening one after the other, therefore offering scope to adjust to the changing environment.

It means that mood is a normal response and is influenced by an individual's environment, life events, and personal history.

When Moods Become Mood Disorders

Everyone experiences mood swings once in a while. They are, after all, a response to our environment. An event with a high emotional charge - losing a wallet, getting a promotion, failing an exam, being rejected by a lover or achieving a lifelong dream - all these can cause our moods to swing in either direction.

Mood swings are sudden changes in emotional state. Although they seem to come out of nowhere, they are usually triggered by specific factors. Many physical, mental and environmental factors cause shifts in moods. Whether it's a heated argument with a spouse or a stressful event at work, sometimes it's difficult to identify what causes the mood swings.

Lifestyle factors like diet, exercise, hormones, and sleep can significantly influence our mood. For example, having low levels of iron, zinc, magnesium, and omega-3 fatty acids in your diet is often associated with lowered energy and a bad mood. Eating a poor-quality diet high in sugary desserts, fried food, and high-fat dairy products can lead to a depressive state in some cases.

Psychological and environmental factors, traumatic events, toxic relationships, or problems at work that are associated with negative emotions can influence our mood.

Hormonal changes can cause mood swings. Women experience changes in their hormones as a part of their menstrual cycle. They experience it during PMS (premenstrual syndrome) one or two weeks before their period and around menopause. Symptoms can include depression, mood swings, headaches, bloating, etc.

Although mood swings are harmless, if they become a regular occurrence and happen abruptly for seemingly no apparent reason, this can indicate mental health conditions and mood disorders like depression, anxiety or bipolar disorder, for which you may need to see a mental health professional for medical advice.

Whatever the cause, here are a few things you can do if you notice mood shifts frequently.

1. Identify

Become mindful of when you experience mood swings and mood changes, how severe they are, and what is their apparent cause.

We can get so caught up with our lives that we can sometimes miss paying attention to what we are feeling. Therefore, become mindful of your emotional state. Refusing to look at something will not generally solve it.

Notice how often and how severe are the mood shifts. Becoming aware of the duration of the mood will help you understand your mood cycles.

Try to identify any apparent reasons for the mood swings. It could be due to

1. Lack of proper diet rich in micronutrients. If you are on a diet program and experience mood swings, please consult your nutritionist.
2. Lack of sleep is one of the leading causes of mood swings in the present day. As we explore sleep in this book in the second section, we will explore if you are in sleep debt and how to deal with it.
3. Hormonal changes can trigger mood swings. If that is so, notice any changes the body is going through and consult a doctor.
4. Environmental factors like an argument, a long-standing relationship problem, finances, or health can contribute to bad moods for more extended periods.

5. Moon cycles affect moods too. The moon affects water; we all know that. Emotions are water energy. Hence, moods can fluctuate with moon cycles. Pay attention and study yourself if this is so.

Once you identify your symptoms, you may start taking action and seeing positive shifts in your life.

2. Do some research

We live in a day and age when information is readily available at our fingertips. At the same time, misinformation is also abundant. Use your common sense and filters when reading about this online.

Connect with doctors and friends to know more about moods and mood swings. If you wish to educate yourself about mood swings, use reputable sources that rely on solid scientific evidence, leave no room for subjective interpretations, or speak to a professional.

3. Be kind to yourself

If you are a sensitive individual who feels more than others, it's not a disease or something terrible. That's just how your nervous system is tuned. Even if you are not a sensitive individual and are experiencing mood swings, please seek out help.

Do not be unkind to yourself and torture yourself into not feeling something. It's human to feel. Listen to your feelings and moods. You will need to establish a balance between going with your moods and then sometimes pulling yourself out of it, too. Knowing what to do when comes with establishing a good relationship with self.

4. Seek out help

If your mood swings are severe, prolonged, more than frequent and such that they interfere with your day-to-day functioning, it is time to seek out help from a professional who can accurately diagnose the underlying condition.

A psychiatrist will prescribe medications to help you manage any mental health disorder. They also typically are trained in therapeutic approaches to help you cope.

For people with psychiatric disorders, their mood swings are likely caused by their genetics and because of developmental experiences[8] too (think nature and nurture). It is widely recognised that depressive and anxious disorders are often triggered by life events, which means the depressed and anxious mood would be a normal (healthy) response to the environment and stress. This proves that depression and anxiety are not just problems of the individual brain, but are consequences of how individuals' brains respond to the stressors in the environment[7].

Psychologists can offer psychotherapy to help with mood disorders that can provide support, education, therapeutic help for helping shift the response to stressors and guidance to you and/or your family to help you function better and increase your well-being.

It is better to reach out to a therapeutic coach or a psychologist when you notice mood swings becoming more frequent no matter what the reason is.

Final thoughts on moods

Moods, just like emotions, attune us to our environment. A positive mood makes us notice more of good things in our life, whereas, a negative mood brings to our notice things that are annoying or a threat. For example, the experience of travel depends on the mood. When one is in a positive mood, one may enjoy the journey, scenery and food on the way. But in a negative mood, the same travel may feel like a punishment, with a hurry to reach the destination, finding fault with the food and facilities on the way.

Moods are a normal part of being human. And the best way to handle them is through acceptance. Emotional reactions to situations are natural and it's just as natural for those reactions to turn into moods over time.

But an important thing to remember is that just as nothing is permanent in life, so is true for moods. They too shall pass. Becoming aware of how our moods affect our thinking and decision-making can help us handle them better.

CHAPTER FOUR

MIND-BODY CONNECTION

"Our bodies change our minds, and our minds change our behaviour, and our behaviour changes our outcomes."
— Amy Cuddy

Our mind and body are intricately connected. The body affects the mind, and how we think is reflected in how our body behaves. Our body reacts to everything we think and speak.

The lemon experiment proves this very clearly:

Imagine a lovely bright yellow lemon. Hold it in your hands and notice the coolness of its skin. Now imagine taking a knife and cutting this lemon in half. As you cut, the juice flows on your fingers, and you can smell that distinct citrus aroma. Take the half and squeeze a few drops on your tongue and suck on this piece.

Perhaps just reading this has your mouth salivating.

But there is no real lemon. And yet, your body responded as if there was a real lemon.

The mind doesn't know the difference between imagination and reality. If it can imagine something clearly, the body experiences it as well. This is why, whether we experience an event or simply imagine one, our brain reacts similarly in both instances, and plenty of scientific studies prove this.

When there is a perception of an emotional event (real or imagined), the brain releases chemicals like cortisol (stress response) or oxytocin (pleasure/love response). These chemicals don't just affect our brain but flow through our body, influencing bodily functions.

Stress response releases cortisol, which elevates the heartbeat, pulse and blood pressure and makes the blood flow into the arms and legs to activate and assist the fight or flight response. Thus, the mind commands the body into a physical reaction. This is called the '**psychosomatic response**'.

Similarly, how you use your body impacts your mind, emotions, confidence and sense of relaxation. This is called the '**somatopsychic response**'. Placing chopsticks or a pen in your mouth horizontally forces your face into a smile. This affects the mind into emulating a happiness response and lowering stress in the body.

We all know about body language and how physiology affects the mental state. High power poses increase testosterone levels by almost twenty percent[9].

It's amazing how our body responds to the way we think and feel about ourselves and the world around us. Just think about what your posture is like when you are feeling low and depressed. Your body is slumped, bent, bloated (for some) and you feel like you are dragging yourself. Now notice how your body behaves when you are optimistic, happy and enthusiastic – your posture is upright, shoulders stretched back, and when you walk, it seems like you are gliding. There is a spring in your step and a beaming radiance on your face.

That means we need to be very careful of how we talk about our body and what we think about it. But on the bright side - we can shift how we feel by simply changing our thoughts.

We are what we think

The mind has two parts - Conscious and Subconscious. If the subconscious mind is the ocean, the conscious mind is a small island in this ocean. At any given moment, the mind is receiving 2-4 million bits of information from the environment. The subconscious mind is taking all that in. But our conscious mind is handling only 5-7 bits of information from that.

This gives us a perspective on how vast the subconscious is and how small the conscious thinking mind is. We are never conscious of everything at the same time. For example, were you aware of the nail on the little toe in your left foot until you read this?

You are reading this book with your conscious mind and perhaps thinking of one or two more things consciously. But your subconscious mind is receiving and registering so much more - the feel of the book or device on which you are reading in your hands, connecting the information you are receiving to that which you already hold, the temperature in the room, the sensation of what you are wearing on your body, the air pressure around you and so much more besides its usual work of making the body's organs work.

All the information you receive is sorted and filtered through certain criteria in your mind - shape, size, history, previous experience, collective thought, etc. It is being stacked in ways that can make sense to you. Some information is also being deleted to make the environment and information more manageable for the conscious mind. For example, you can always see your nose in your peripheral vision, but your brain edits this information out.

> “*“A lot of what our senses are doing is something like data compression: simplifying, in order to be able to function,” says Mazviita Chirimuuta at the University of Pittsburgh in Pennsylvania.*”

This sorting is done through learned behaviours and experiences. Suppose you have learnt that doing something new is exciting and adventurous. In that case, the prospect of it will be sorted into a positive experience. But if new or different experiences have been full of anxiety and discomfort for you in the past, then this same experience in the present will be sorted into something that is negative and needs to be avoided. This kind of sorting is happening constantly for every person, experience or thing.

This means we can never look at the world objectively but always subjectively in terms of our past experiences and learnings.

> “*“A human being is a part of the whole called by us universe, a part limited in time and space. He experiences himself, his thoughts and feeling as something separated from the rest, a kind of optical delusion of his consciousness. This delusion is a kind of prison for us, restricting us to our personal*

desires and to affection for a few persons nearest to us. Our task must be to free ourselves from this prison by widening our circle of compassion to embrace all living creatures and the whole of nature in its beauty."

— Albert Einstein "

Whenever a piece of information comes in through the senses into the brain, the mind sorts it, and according to the meaning assigned to it (threat or not), it signals the response in terms of emotions. If the information is sorted as good, happy emotions are produced, and the body gets into the appropriate action. If it is sorted as harmful or threatening, then stressful or negative emotions are produced, and an appropriate response is initiated - fight, flight, crying, shouting, etc.

Shifting and changing these filters (also commonly known as lenses or perspectives) helps in re-calibrating what the mind processes as a threat or not. You will find many techniques in the book's second part that can help you do that.

CHAPTER FIVE

FOUR HAPPY HORMONES

"When a monkey loses a banana to a rival, he feels bad, but he doesn't expand the problem by thinking about it over and over. He looks for another banana. He ends up feeling rewarded rather than harmed. Humans use their extra neurons to construct theories about bananas and end up constructing pain."

— Loretta Graziano Breuning, Habits of a Happy Brain

Environment triggers our response – good or bad. More precisely, our perception of the environment is responsible for our emotional and behavioural response to it. Between perceiving situations and responding to them, chemicals called neurotransmitters and hormones play a vital role.

They help your brain understand, evaluate and communicate what you are experiencing. Each of these chemicals has a specific job - they activate in a certain way, signal certain emotions and stimulate different areas of the brain.

In your journey of managing and healing emotions and moods and finding happiness, these are the chemicals that will help you. We will explore each of these four chemicals, their role and how to activate them.

There are four happy hormones or chemicals:

1. Serotonin
2. Dopamine
3. Endorphins
4. Oxytocin

Serotonin - For Good Moods

When you are feeling happy and everything feels right in the world, you are feeling the effects of serotonin. Serotonin, also known as **happy chemical**, is a natural mood stabiliser and booster[10]. It helps with mood, sleep, digestion, nausea, wound healing, bone health, blood clotting and sexual desire.

The following things help to increase serotonin:

1. Exposure to outdoors and sunlight
2. Exercise and body movement
3. Eating a well-balanced diet of proteins and carbohydrates,
4. Consuming foods rich in tryptophan (nuts, seeds, eggs, cheese, turkey, pineapple)
5. Dietary supplements
6. Practice meditation and mindfulness

Dopamine - The Reward Chemical

Dopamine, also called the 'feel-good' hormone or the 'reward chemical', gives you feelings of pleasure, satisfaction and motivation. It plays a role in controlling memory, mood, sleep, learning, concentration, movement and other body functions[11].

The high that you feel when you achieve something or do something fun, comes from an increase in dopamine in the brain. Too little dopamine can contribute to depression. Because it's a reward and pleasure chemical, excess of it plays a role in addictions.

Dopamine is part of your reward system. From an evolutionary standpoint, this system rewards you when you do what you need to do to survive — eat, drink, compete to survive and reproduce. Our brains are hard-wired to seek out behaviours that release dopamine in our reward system. When you're doing something pleasurable, a large amount of dopamine is released into your system. You feel good and you seek more of that feeling.

This is why junk food and sugar are so addictive. They trigger the release of a large amount of dopamine into your brain, which gives you the feeling that you're on top of the world and you want to repeat that experience.

Here are some simple things you can do to harness dopamine:

1. Do something creative
2. Try something new, something that makes you happy
3. Listen to music
4. Set realistic goals and achieve them
5. Complete a task
6. Tick something off your bucket list

7. Eat food rich in magnesium and tryosin (dairy foods, avocados, apples, poultry, seeds)

Endorphins - The Pain reliever

Endorphins are the body's natural pain killers. They help you overcome stress and discomfort and improve your sense of well-being. This hormone is released by the body in response to pain or stress. Endorphins also tend to be released when engaged in pleasurable activities such as eating, sex and exercise.

Endorphins promote memory and cognitive health, boost self-esteem, reduce inflammation and support a healthy immune system. Endorphins dull the pain and can produce a "high" that is both healthy and safe.

Here are a few things you can do to increase endorphins in the body:

1. Exercise, workout, do yoga, running - any form of physical activity that brings you pleasure
2. Laughter
3. Meditation
4. Sex
5. Sunshine
6. Certain foods increase endorphins, like dark chocolate
7. Hot water bath

Oxytocin - The Love Hormone

Oxytocin is a hormone that manages some important aspects of the female and male reproductive system as well as aspects of human behaviour. This hormone facilitates childbirth and helps us bond with loved ones[12]. Our bodies produce oxytocin when we are excited by our love partner and when we fall in love, hence the "love hormone" and "cuddle hormone".

Oxytocin reduces anxiety levels, helps build trust and improves overall psychological stability. Some of this hormone's relationship-enhancing effects are trust, empathy, positive relationship memories, fidelity, positive communication etc.

When you're attracted to someone, your brain releases dopamine, your serotonin levels increase, and oxytocin is produced. This causes you to feel a surge of positive emotion and everything feels beautiful.

Natural ways to enhance oxytocin are:

1. Hug someone you love
2. Show love and affection
3. Spend time with friends
4. Do something nice for someone
5. Give a massage, cuddle, make love
6. Workout
7. Listen to music
8. Share a laugh

CHAPTER SIX

Paving the Way to a Happier You

The journey of healing is not about erasing emotions but about developing a healthier relationship with them. It's about learning to weather the storms with grace, finding the calm within the chaos, and equipping yourself with tools to help you on this healing path.

In the following pages, I share techniques and methods to handle not just emotions and moods, but also the kind of lifestyle and daily rituals that you can develop that will help you find harmony in the emotional ups and downs. My aim is not just to give you bandaids but also to prepare you to navigate the landscape of emotions.

Emotions are a part of our life and will always be. There will be times when we are in a good mental and physical state. In such times, it is relatively easier to deal with emotions, but when it is not so, that is when we need all the help from both physical and spiritual realms to find inner peace.

A good place to begin your journey of this healing is to have the intent to heal. Intention is very important as it clears the path and provides the necessary energy to deal with any difficulties. Before you proceed, take a moment to quieten your mind and get a sense of your body and mind – is it open to healing? Are you ready to heal?

If the answer is a resounding yes, then go ahead. But if it is not a clear yes, ask yourself what you are gaining by not healing or letting go of what is no longer needed. Books, therapists and coaches can help you find the right path and give you the best tools, but it is you who has to take the journey. If you are willing to open up and explore healing at your own pace, if you want to take the healing journey to help you open up to healing yourself, then that is also an excellent place to start.

In the following pages, I have talked about two aspects of handling and healing moods and emotions

1. Physiological - through the body
2. Spiritual - through the mind and soul

Although we need both worlds – physical and energetic – to survive, I have divided the techniques into these two categories for the sake of ease and to help you find harmony between the tools from both aspects.

We nourish ourselves with physical means every day through food, sleep, exercise, etc. We also need to nourish ourselves energetically through learning, meditation, energy care and so on. We experience the world through our physical senses but interpret it through the mind, which is of the energy world.

It is always a good idea to use tools from both aspects simultaneously because the mind and body work together in harmony. The mind influences the body and vice versa. Anything that influences the mind will eventually impact the body, and anything that affects the body will influence the mind.

You can use these methods individually or in combination that feels right for you to uplift your spirits and let the energy flow in your body.

Part II

Techniques to Handle Emotions and Moods

Physiology
Honouring the body

CHAPTER SEVEN

FOOD

Only 5% of Serotonin (happiness chemical) is made in the brain. The other 95% is made in the gut.

How often have you reached out for comfort food when you feel low, emotionally overwhelmed or down?

Food possesses a distinctive ability to trigger emotions and memories. It is so deeply associated with feeling good that it can remind us of positive memories from childhood. When the food critic Anton Ego from the animated movie Ratatouille is served the so-called "peasant dish" ratatouille, he is instantly reminded of his mother's love and cooking. It brings a smile of nostalgia to his face and brings life back to him, whose office had the shadows of a coffin.

Many people struggle with cravings and food addictions because of this very reason - comfort. It fulfils a need for soothing emotions when nothing else does. But seeking soothing and comfort from food can pull one down in a dangerous spiral.

Many comfort foods we resort to are unhealthy and full of chemicals and preservatives. They are usually made of refined flour and sugar, along with chemicals. They provide a high for the moment, but when the high wears down, the lows are even deeper. It can result in an unhealthy relationship with food, leading to food disorders and obesity.

To use food in a manner that's healthy, soothing, uplifting and nourishing, and in a way that helps with harmonising moods and emotions, we need to build a better relationship with food and understand the rituals of consuming food.

"*"You are what you eat."*"

Food and Vibrations

We are energy beings, made of life force energy, and we need energy for sustenance and good health. This energy is consumed through food, water and air.

Food contains energy (commonly measured through calories), which means it also has a vibration.

Notice how you feel after eating a bag of chips versus when you eat fruits or a fresh salad. Processed foods are very low in vibration and do not provide your body with the adequate energy or vibration it needs to function at its optimal level. On the other hand, fresh foods are very high in vibration and provide your body with energy and vibrancy.

High vibrations help to create and maintain the internal energy of the body. Research has discovered that our body heals and repairs itself when vibration is at a certain rate and frequency.

High Vibrational Foods:

- Organic fruits and vegetables
- Herbs and spices
- Pure or filtered water
- Healthy oils such as olive oil, avocado and coconut
- Nuts and seeds
- Fermented foods
- Raw chocolate
- Raw honey and maple syrup
- Legumes
- Whole grains such as buckwheat, rice, millets or amaranth

Low Vibrational Foods:

- Genetically modified (GMO) food, and conventional food that has been treated with chemicals and pesticides
- Artificial sugars and sweeteners
- Soda and high-sugar fruit juices
- Alcohol
- Processed, packaged and fast foods
- Unhealthy oils such as canola and rapeseed
- Deep-fried and microwaved foods
- Meat, fish and poultry
- Frozen food

Natural food that is minimally or not at all processed is high-vibrational. The more you process food, the lower its vibration becomes. Remember, if it comes in a packet, it has low vibrations. If what you eat doesn't grow naturally in that form, it is low in vibration.

Why Is High-Vibrational Food Important?

Emotions have vibrations, and so does food. We read about the vibrations and frequencies of emotions in the first chapter. The body is very well connected with the mind. Low vibrational thoughts and emotions lower the vibrations of the body, producing energy blocks, lowered emotional and mental states and eventually diseases. High vibrational thoughts and emotions create happiness in the mind and contribute to a healthy body.

Similarly, low-vibrational foods lower the vibration of the body and mind and create more low-vibrational energies/emotions and vice versa.

For example, if you suffer from depression, the energy of the body is already in a lowered state. If you eat packaged foods, processed food and very little fresh food, you are not feeding higher vibrational energies to your body. The low vibrational food will lower your energies even more, adding to the depressive states.

This is why food plays such an essential role in raising your vibrations. It helps shift the energy of the body from within. And your body will thank you for taking care of it by helping you feel better. When yogis perform their rituals and sadhana, they eat Saatvic food to uplift their vibrations, which will help their spiritual practices.

How To Make Food High Vibrational

1. **Prepare food with love and a positive intention.** Food cooked with love is high in vibration and healing properties, whereas if the person cooking is feeling stressed or frustrated, it lowers the vibration of the food.
2. **Consume your meals sitting down**, with a peaceful mind and in a positive energetic space. Environment matters, this is why we decorate the dining areas with beautiful pictures of fruit bowls and lavishly laid tables. Live plants also raise the vibration of the space where you consume food.
3. **Say a prayer before eating and bless the food.** The prayer could be anything - mantra, chant, affirmation or simply a few heartfelt words. Dr Masaru Emoto's research that our words and thoughts affect water has proven that thoughts and intentions change the vibrations of water as well as food[13].
4. **Do not overcook food.** Cooking reduces the vibrational frequency of food. Raw foods have the highest vibrations. Cooked fruits and vegetables have lower vibration. Try to include as much raw food in your diet as possible.
5. **Use energy healing.** Touch your food with your bare hands (make sure you wash your hands before doing this). Your hands have the healing touch, and your vibrations and thoughts are transferred into food when you touch it. If you are trained in any energy healing system like Reiki, you can reiki your food before and/or after cooking.

Eating Rituals

Most of the older cultures have rituals around food and eating. This is also why food is a big part of any religious or spiritual celebration. Ayurveda, the ancient science of health, describes in detail what kind of food suits which individual based on their *doshas* and Prakriti (*Vata, Pitta, Kapha)* and ideal times and seasons to eat particular foods.

Each *dosha* affects how an individual experiences and responds to the environment. For example, those governed by *Vata dosha* have variable and changeable emotions. They tend to have more fears and phobias. *Pitta* prakriti people tend to be active and dynamic and more prone to irritability and anger. *Kapha*-type people are slow to respond to stimulus, generally smiling and very few things seem to make them angry[14].

Since the *doshas* affect both mind and body, it makes sense to eat according to it. Though you can find out your Prakriti through questionnaires online, it is best to consult an Ayurvedic doctor because it is a very subtle system.

No matter what your *dosha is*, there are a few things you can adopt when eating food, almost like a ritual, that will improve the vibrations of what you are consuming and how it will be processed in the body. One of the most important rituals is to honour your food. Here is one way to do that.

Honour the food you eat. Say a prayer, and express gratitude for all the hands that brought the food to you. You could either create your prayer or start with one from Bhagavad Gita, the ancient Hindu scripture.

"ब्रह्मार्पणं ब्रह्म हविर्ब्रह्माग्नौ ब्रह्मणा हुतम् ।
ब्रह्मैव तेन गन्तव्यं ब्रह्मकर्मसमाधिना ॥ ४-२४॥

brahma-arpaṇaṁ brahma haviḥ brahma-agnau brahmaṇā hutam

brahma ēva tēna gantavyam brahma-karma-samādhinā. (Gita 04-24)

The act of offering is Brahman.The offering itself is Brahman.

The offering is done by Brahman in the sacred fire which is Brahman.

He alone attains Brahman, who, in all actions, is fully absorbed in Brahman."

Some other rituals that you can imbibe in your daily life are:

1. **Try to include all 6 tastes in a meal**. Begin with something sweet like jaggery. According to Ayurveda, when you begin with sweet, it overpowers the *vayu.* Thensour and salty stimulate the digestive fire, followed by pungent, bitter and astringent to subdue *kapha.* Ideally, start with sweet like jaggery and end with astringent like betel nut or kattha (acacia).
2. **Offer the first bite to God or the Universe.** Keep aside the first bite of the food as an offering to God. This is a way of telling the universe that this food comes from it and goes into it. It's a way of expressing gratitude to the Source.
3. **Be mindful while eating.** Eat slowly and with all your senses. Avoid distractions like TV or mobile while you eat. It is about respecting what you eat because what goes inside you will nourish you. Use your hands while handling food, your sense of smell enhances the flavour as well as tells your body what's good for you and what's

not. Also, when you eat mindfully, you won't overeat.

4. **Chew your food properly enough times.** Don't just gulp it down. The less you chew, the more your stomach will have to work on it. Also, the mouth has certain enzymes that are not present in the stomach that help break down the food.
5. **Breathe in between bites.** When you don't breathe in between bites, you will feel bloated by the end of the meal. Breathing gives you and your mind a tiny break. This break is essential because it helps you assess the taste of the food, how it feels and whether your stomach is full or not. Use this time to notice the environment and the ambience. Become mindful of your body as you eat.

Some Do's and Don'ts of eating

- Eat as fresh as possible.
- Eat when you are hungry
- Eat seasonal food only
- Don't talk too much while having food.
- Don't drink a lot of water during and immediately after having food.
- Wash hands and mouth before and after meal
- Don't take a shower or hard exercise immediately after having food.
- Sit in Vajrasana/diamond position after a meal
- Don't eat until your stomach is stuffed. Leave some space for digestion
- Don't lie down immediately after food

The 3 Gunas

In Yoga and Ayurveda, 3 *Gunas* are a way to classify the quality of energy. These *gunas* are *Sattva, Rajas,* and *Tamas.*

Sattva or *Sattvic* is balanced, harmony, purity, health and wellbeing.

Rajas or *Rajasic* is activity, restlessness, stress and anger.

Tamas or *Tamasic* means lethargy, dullness and laziness.

There is a proportion of each *Guna* inside us. Without Tamas, we would not sleep; without Rajas, we would lack dynamism; and without Sattva, life would be uninspiring and without the higher human qualities. Foods are also classified into these three categories.

Sattvic Food

Sattvic food is known for its purity, lightness and positive energy. It is high in *Prana* or the life force energy, enhances mental and physical clarity and creates peace and harmony. This is a plant-based diet consisting of foods, fruits and vegetables, whole grains, nuts, seeds, legumes, some spices like ginger and fennel etc. In essence, it is minimally processed and cooked, with few spices and free of additives and preservatives.

This food is easy to digest, light on the stomach and abundant in nutrients. It facilitates mental clarity, spiritual growth and practices, balances *doshas*, heightens consciousness and enhances mental and emotional well-being.

Rajasic Food

Rajasic food is known for its luxury, spiciness and flavour. It awakens the senses and evokes passion and ambition. Examples of Rajasic foods are deep-fried items, strongly flavoured dishes, tea, coffee, chocolate etc.

Rajasic food has intense flavours; it delights the taste buds but can be heavy and difficult to digest. It invigorates the mind and body and prompts it into action. However excessive consumption can lead to restlessness, irritability, anger and acidity. It gives an initial burst of energy, but eventually, one experiences a dip in energy and an increase in stress levels.

Tamasic Food

Tamasic food is least favourable because it is heavy, has a dulling effect and can harm health. Processed and stale food with no nutritional value, food with high preservatives, white flour, white sugar, excessive meat, fish and alcohol, onions, mushrooms, and microwaved food are considered tamasic food.

Tamasic food is heavy, greasy, challenging to digest, and lacks nutrients. Consumed in excess, it dulls the mind, encourages destructive emotions and behaviour, increases sluggishness and lethargy and causes health issues.

It is essential to consume food according to time, age and circumstances. All kinds of foods are needed, but everything in balance is important. Know your body, and what you are experiencing in the present and eat accordingly.

Certain Foods that can help with lifting moods and emotions

Certain foods have been known to improve brain health and boost your moods as well. Before you proceed to read the list, remember that healthy doesn't have to mean tasteless. So here is a list of healthy foods that can help you feel good.

1. Bananas

Bananas are a great source of vitamin B6, which helps in synthesizing neurotransmitters like dopamine and serotonin, responsible for making us feel good. They contain about 16 grams of sugar, which is released slowly into the bloodstream, leading to better mood stability and stable blood sugar levels. As bananas are high in Kapha dosha, it's best to consume them during the daytime.

2. Fermented Foods

Fermented foods like yoghurt, idlis, dhokla, kimchi, buttermilk, lentil pancakes, etc., improve gut health, which is directly related to moods. Fermentation creates probiotics, which are great for gut health. Serotonin, a neurotransmitter that affects mood, stress response and appetite is produced by your gut microbiome. But only naturally fermented foods that are not processed too much have this quality.

3. Nuts and seeds

Nuts and seeds are high in plant-based proteins, healthy fats, and fibre. They also provide the amino acids that produce mood-boosting serotonin. What's more, a 10-year study in 15,980 people linked moderate nut intake to a 23%

lower risk of depression[15]. Almonds, cashews, walnuts, and peanuts, as well as pumpkin, sesame, and sunflower seeds, are your new best friends.

4. Beans and lentils

High in fibre and plant-based proteins, beans and lentils are an excellent source of B vitamins, zinc, magnesium and selenium. All these nutrients are associated with good mental and physical health. B vitamins help increase mood booster neurotransmitters and even help lower the risk of depression.

5. Dark chocolate

When it comes to moods, chocolates can't be far behind. It helps increase blood flow to the brain, reduce inflammation and improve brain health, all of which support mood regulation. Even smelling chocolate produces feel-good chemicals. But remember to consume it in limited quantities since it's a high-calorie food.

Avoid too much caffeine (coffee, chocolates) as they give you a high initially but plunge the moods further into depression later. Eat less refined carbohydrates like candy, cookies, and white flour. The golden rule is "eat often and eat light."

Some other mood boosters are fresh fruits and vegetables (avoid frozen ones), legumes, oranges and salmon. Vitamin B12 helps boost moods. It is normally found in milk and milk products besides non-vegetarian food. For vegans, it is advised to eat B12-fortified foods.

CHAPTER EIGHT

SLEEP

If you didn't know what sleep was, and you had only seen it in a science fiction movie, you would think it was weird and tell all your friends about the movie you'd seen.

They had these people, you know? And they would walk around all day and be OK? And then, once a day, usually after dark, they would lie down on these special platforms and become unconscious. They would stop functioning almost completely, except deep in their minds they would have adventures and experiences that were completely impossible in real life. As they lay there, completely vulnerable to their enemies, their only movements were to occasionally shift from one position to another; or, if one of the 'mind adventures' got too real, they would sit up and scream and be glad they weren't unconscious anymore. Then they would drink a lot of coffee.'

So, next time you see someone sleeping, make believe you're in a science fiction movie. And whisper, 'The creature is regenerating itself."

— George Carlin, Brain Droppings

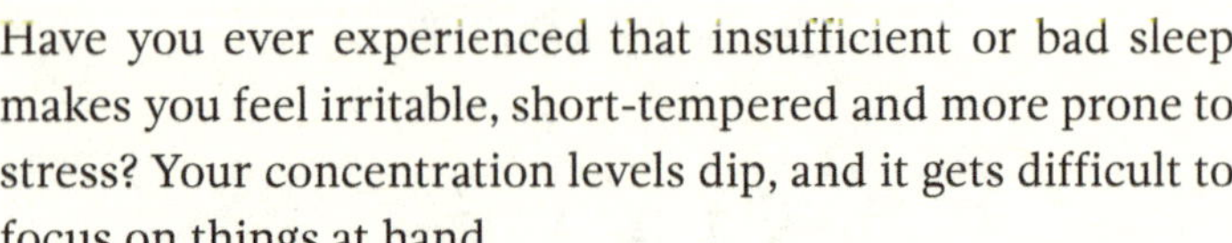

Have you ever experienced that insufficient or bad sleep makes you feel irritable, short-tempered and more prone to stress? Your concentration levels dip, and it gets difficult to focus on things at hand.

A few such nights at a stretch can cause you to overreact to things, life feels like there is nothing too interesting, and your productivity decreases. It almost feels like you are running on low battery.

After experiencing only 4.5 hours of sleep for a week, participants in a study conducted by researchers from the University of Pennsylvania reported feeling more stressed, angry, sad, and mentally exhausted. However, when the subjects returned to their normal sleep routine, they reported a significant improvement in their mood.

Sleep affects how well you think, react, work, learn and interact with others. It is a natural medicine and a repair and maintenance time for the body when some major functions of restoration happen.

Sleep is vital for healthy brain function and maintenance of the physical body. It affects your heart and circulatory system, metabolism, respiratory system, immune system, etc.

Breaking Down the Science of Sleep

There are two phases of sleep - REM and non-REM. REM means rapid eye movement. Non-REM sleep is followed by a short cycle of REM sleep. There are four to six such cycles every night.

Non-Rem sleep is when the brain waves are slowest. During the deep stages of non-REM sleep, the body repairs and regrows tissues, builds bone and muscle and strengthens the immune system.

REM sleep is when the brain is active; dreaming happens in this stage of sleep. This is important because it stimulates the areas of the brain that help with learning and is associated with increased production of proteins. In this stage, the brain sorts through stuff, creating long-term memories and throwing out garbage.

The amount of sleep you need depends on your age and physical activity. The norm is that children need 9-10 hours of sleep, whereas adults need around 8 hours, but this can vary in individuals. Studies also show that women need more sleep than men. Lack of sleep in women can throw their hormones off balance.

If you have missed sleep in the previous days, you will need more sleep to compensate. Similar to being overdrawn at a bank, if you do not get enough sleep, you will incur a "sleep debt". Eventually, your body will require you to pay off the debt.

Sleep-Debt

Long-term lack of sleep can lead to a higher sleep debt. We cannot adapt to less sleep than we need. We may get used to a schedule that doesn't let us have enough sleep, but it gradually affects our judgment, reaction time, and other functions.

Signs of Sleep Debt

Some of the signs of sleep debt are[26]:

1. Feeling drowsy or falling asleep during the day, especially during calm activities like sitting in a movie theatre
2. Short periods of sleep during waking hours (microsleeps)
3. Needing an alarm clock to wake up on time every day
4. Feeling groggy when you wake up in the morning or throughout the day (sleep inertia)
5. Having a hard time getting out of bed every day
6. Mood changes
7. Forgetfulness
8. Trouble focusing on a task
9. Sleeping more on days when you don't have to get up at a certain time

Consequences of Sleep Debt

Sleep debt doesn't show its symptoms at once but gradually the body and mind begin to show the effects of lack of sleep. Some of the symptoms that may begin to show up are:

- Feel tired throughout the day
- Lack of focus and lowered efficiency during the day
- Weak immune system
- Difficulty in processing and storing new information by the brain
- Chronic health problems like heart problems, diabetes, obesity etc.
- Mood disorders like anxiety, depression etc.
- Reduced empathy and emotional recognition, therefore lack of understanding between partners leading to

conflict in relationships
- Decreased ability to respond to insulin
- Increased consumption of food, especially fatty, sweet, and salty foods
- Decreased physical activity

Sleepless nights for an extended period of time can wreak havoc with the body and its circadian rhythm.

Sleep and Moods

There is a two-way relationship between sleep and mood swings – not enough sleep affects your mood, and your mood affects how much and how well you sleep. However, the effect of sleep quality on your mood is much more significant than vice versa[16].

Sleep deprivation increases the negative moods and emotions like anger, irritability, frustration and sadness and decreases the positive emotions. Chronic insomnia can increase the risk of developing a mood disorder, such as depression or anxiety[27].

People who are depressed or anxious often have trouble with sleep[17]. Anxiety and stress keep your body and mind awake and alert and prevent them from going into a restful state. It doesn't let your brain turn off so you can stop thinking and sleep. Lack of sleep adds to the depression or anxiety. This cycle keeps feeding itself until it is broken consciously.

> *"People who have problems with sleep are at increased risk for developing emotional disorders, depression, and anxiety."*
> *-Dr. Lawrence J. Epstein*

One of the important questions in therapy is "Are you sleeping well?"

How to Recover from Sleep Debt and Sleep Better

Incurring sleep debt may be unavoidable in the modern age due to such high demands on our time every day. However, that does not mean we cannot recover from it. Here are some of the ways that can help you recover your sleep debt and help you sleep better. You can use all, one or some of them in a healthy mix. Choose what resonates with you and leave what doesn't. However, if one tip attracts your attention, do consider it.

1. Change your relationship with sleep.

Consider asking yourself,

- What does sleep mean for you?
- What does night-time mean for you?
- What emotions or memories are associated with sleep and night?
- How were you put to sleep - was it a form of punishment, through fear or with bedtime stories?

Answers to these questions can point you in the direction of solutions to your sleep problems. Consider consulting a therapist to deal with some of these issues.

Note: Using sleeping pills to help you sleep is not the best idea in the long run. It can help you sleep, but in the long run, it can be addictive, leaving you in a state where you can't sleep without it at all. Try using them as an aid for some time to help you relax enough so that your body and mind learn to relax and go into sleep mode without sleeping pills. Remember to use this only with a doctor's prescription.

2. Make your bedroom warm and inviting for sleep.

Your bedroom should be inviting and relaxing for you. It should have the vibes of rest and peace. Here are a few things you can do to create that warm, inviting space.

- Use heavy curtains to block out light for complete darkness. The pineal gland needs total darkness to release Melatonin, which aids in sleep. If heavy curtains are not possible, use an eye mask.
- Keep the temperature comfortable enough around room temperature. Heat can interfere with your ability to drift into deep sleep, as can cold.
- Make your bedroom clutter-free. Don't have random things lying around visible. Have a place for everything and everything in its place. Yes, clutter inside wardrobes or drawers is also clutter. So, consider sorting that out too.
- Create your bedroom that is Vaastu compliant or Feng Shui it. Some general tips are -

    - Don't sleep under a beam. If it is unavoidable, hang a crystal there to deflect energies.
    - Don't have a mirror reflecting you while you sleep. It's considered bad for health.
    - Don't have a heavy cabinet above your head as it weighs on your mind.

    - Make sure there are no sharp edges in terms of open shelves facing you. If there are, cover them with a cloth, curtain or a door.
    - Sleep with your head towards the south direction for a good sleep. Avoid having the head in the east or north.

- Use warm or soft colours in the bedroom like lavender or off-white. They relax your mind and make it easier for you to fall asleep. Avoid red, gold or a bright shade for walls or curtains. Bright colours can stimulate energy and cause you to feel more energetic. If you are fond of those colours, use them in cushions or sheets that can be taken off at night.
- Use warm lights or have options for dim lights in the bedroom. They put you in a relaxed state.
- Avoid having any major electronics in the bedroom like TV, computer or a laptop.

3. Avoid working in your bed.

Your bedroom should be associated with rest instead of active work energies. This is especially true for the bed. It is said that if you work sitting in bed, it weakens your Jupiter and creates blocks to success in career and financial growth according to astrology. Also, you are causing conflict in two opposite energies - rest and active work (mental work is also active work). This can cause you to lose your sleep as well as be bad for your performance and efficiency at work.

4. Food that can help and what to avoid

There are certain foods and drinks that can help you with sleep. The age-old wisdom of having warm milk just before bedtime still holds. You can have milk or turmeric milk for its added benefits.

If you are lactose intolerant or vegan, you can try other calming herbal teas like chamomile, which is known for its relaxing properties and is widely recommended for stress relief and insomnia. Besides that, you can also have passionflower tea which is known to help with inflammation and anxiety.

Almonds and walnuts consumed regularly also help with improving the quality of sleep.

What to avoid

Avoid any nervous stimulants like coffee, tea or nicotine. Coffee, tea or any other drink that contains caffeine creates a spike in adrenaline and cortisol in the body. Caffeine is a stimulant that creates more alertness in the body and mind. It also reduces the deep sleep period, which can make you feel unrested or exhausted when you wake up.

Alcohol-induced sleep is not sound or refreshing. It might be helping you sleep, but it is not the sleep that replenishes you. So, avoid alcohol or nicotine before bedtime.

The problem with nervous stimulants like tea and coffee is that they cause a spike in energy levels immediately but later cause a sharper dip than it really should. Consuming too much of these affects the body's ability to store energy. Instead, opt for herbal teas that have a calming effect.

5. Set up a routine and stick to it

Sometimes, we get stuck in a catch-22 situation with routines. The inability to sleep early leads to waking up late, which doesn't let you sleep early again. This dilemma leads one to get stuck in a bad sleep routine. One of the things about a routine is don't think of it as something you HAVE to do. Routine is natural. The Sun has a routine, and so does the Moon and all the other things in the universe. Routine is all about learning to flow in a rhythm.

Consider it like flowing with a river, effortless and natural. If you are stuck in a bad routine, it is also a routine. All you have to do is shift it more closely according to your body clock. Following it may feel more mechanical when you begin, but as your body adapts to it, it feels more natural eventually. This will take time, just like any other habit. But this habit has increasing gains with time.

If you are a night owl, i.e., your energy peaks after sunset, use those hours for productive work. But begin to unwind by 10 PM.

Sleeping by 11 PM is a good idea for the body because according to the Chinese medicine's organ clock, 11 PM is when the Liver and gallbladder begin to regulate chi in the body and metabolise food, fats and experiences. If you miss sleep during this period, your metabolism takes a beating and causes sluggishness in the body.

So, one way to stick to a routine is to wake up at a specific time no matter what time you sleep so that eventually your body learns the new clock. If you feel drowsy during the day, use power naps or Yoga Nidra to help you reduce sleep debt and natural nervous stimulants like refreshing teas and Ash Gourd juice to keep you alert in a better manner.

6. Use essential oils that promote relaxation

Aromatherapy is one of the most underrated healing systems. Our sense of smell is the most potent sense to help us associate routines, memories and people with good or bad feelings. Hence, it makes perfect sense to create a positive anchor with the sense of smell and associate it with relaxation and sleep.

There are also some aromas and herbs that promote relaxation and calmness and have been proven to help with insomnia. Essential oils can be used with air diffusers or applied directly to the skin.

Always remember to use natural essential oils instead of synthetic ones, and avoid perfumes around bedtime, especially strong smells, as they can interfere with sleep.

Here are some essential oils that can help you with sleep and relaxation:

- Lavender oil
- Ylang Ylang oil
- Chamomile oil
- Peppermint oil
- Sandalwood oil
- Clary sage oil
- Vetiver oil
- Eucalyptus oil
- Valerian oil

It comes down to finding what works best for you. Choose one that smells best for you and the one that you like. Remember, the smell should not overwhelm your senses.

7. Meditate

No matter how much you talk about the benefits of meditation, it is never enough. Meditation can help you sleep better. It also helps with having longer periods of nourishing deep sleep.

Choose a method that works best for you. You can choose a guided meditation to help you drift into sleep or focus on your breath to calm your mind. If you are familiar with a healing system like Reiki, practising it while trying to sleep can help you relax deeply and offer the added benefit of healing as you sleep.

Try yoga Nidra to help your mind relax so your body can relax too. This can be done during the day to relax and before bedtime to unwind as well.

8. Don't force yourself to sleep

If you find yourself tossing and turning and unable to sleep, get up and do something relaxing until you are ready to sleep. Read a book, write a journal, meditate or listen to music. Come back to bed when you are ready to sleep.

Don't struggle with sleep. The more you struggle, the more it will elude you. Sometimes, reverse psychology also helps. Tell yourself, "I am not going to sleep tonight", and see if that works for you.

Try taking a warm shower before bedtime to help your body relax.

9. Stay away from electronics

Minimise exposure to blue light from electronics at least 30-40 min before sleep as it inhibits the release of Melatonin which helps you sleep.

Also, the content you consume around bedtime can become the content of your dreams, so pay attention, especially if you suffer from nightmares or are sensitive to dreams and the feelings therein.

Doom scrolling can keep you awake and alert instead of helping you sleep and delays REM sleep. Exposure to social media also creates more anxiety from comparisons.

10. Understand your body

Sleep doesn't have to be a boring task or something you dread. Consider it an act of self-love that you are doing for your mind and body. Begin to create a better relationship with your body so that you can listen to what your body wants and fulfil its needs.

Notice how long it takes for your mind and body to unwind before you can go to sleep. Give yourself that time additionally so it doesn't reduce your sleep timings.

Take light meals in the evening. Heavier meals take time to digest and cause the body to direct a lot of energy to the digestion process. This doesn't let the mind unwind; it can sure make you groggy but won't help you fall asleep.

Drink enough fluids before bed, but not so much that you will have to wake up in between for a trip to the bathroom.

Avoid doing a lot of active work before bedtime as it will raise the level of stress hormones and hinder sleep.

Communicate with the body to learn what will help it to relax and get ready to sleep.

11. Consider the possibility of other factors hindering your sleep

- **Jet lag** - give yourself enough time and sleep for your body to reset its clock
- **Nightmares** - consider seeing a therapist or a spiritual advisor for nightmares
- **Too much stress in the body** - practice calming yoga and exercises before bedtime to help your body release that excess cortisol and help you relax.
- **Overactive mind** - do some journaling, practice hand mudras to help calm your mental energy. If nothing helps, practice breathing exercises to help settle the overthinking.
- **Lack of activity during the day** - you need to assess how much activity you need during the day for you to be sufficiently tired at night to sleep. Remember to give both your mind and body some activity to tire them out enough to sleep.
- **Snoring or sleep apnea** - If snoring doesn't let you have deep sleep, try sleeping on your side. If you have sleep apnea, see a doctor to help you with that. Lack of oxygen in the brain during sleep due to sleep apnea or snoring can leave you feeling groggy in the morning.

CHAPTER NINE

Movement

"Your hand opens and closes and opens and closes. If it were always a fist or always stretched open, you would be paralyzed. Your deepest presence is in every small contracting and expanding, the two as beautifully balanced and coordinated as bird wings."

– Rumi

When you feel anxious, what provides you more relief - sitting or moving around?

Anxiety and stress are energies that tend to create restlessness in the body and mind. Therefore, moving around feels better when you are anxious. This is because when you move and are physically active, it tends to release all the stuck, restless and negative energy in your body and gives it an outlet to move out as well.

You know I am going to talk about the benefits of exercise, or more precisely, movement (groans). But what if movement doesn't have to mean what it has meant to you all these years? By the time you finish reading this section, your views on movement might have changed, helping you let go of the resistance to exercise in its various forms.

Why movement helps

It's a no-brainer that people who exercise regularly have better mental and emotional health and lower rates of psychological and physical illness. Exercise releases endorphins and produces happy chemicals in the body. Happy people are healthy people. Physical activity, whether hitting the gym, taking a stroll with your dog, participating in a sport, or playing with your kids, can uplift your mood and increase your energy levels.

Receiving care and affection from your primary caregivers triggered the release of positive neurotransmitters in your brain, creating a potent blend of chemicals that fostered feelings of safety, love, and pleasure during nurturing interactions. As you mature, this innate need for positive emotional well-being remains ingrained within you. Though exercise does not replicate the soothing feelings of receiving love, it releases the same combination of chemicals (neurotransmitters) that make you feel happy and loved.

This is why physical activity works as an anti-depressant. Exercise changes the levels of serotonin, stress hormones and endorphins in the brain. Chemical reactions in the brain are one of the primary reasons that you feel the brain-boosting benefits of exercise. The endorphins that are produced by the brain during intense exercise cause the brain to respond as positively as they would with euphoric drugs.

The exhilarating feeling you experience after a workout often referred to as a "high," is attributed to the release of chemicals known as Endocannabinoids. These molecules are capable of crossing the blood-brain barrier to bind with neural receptors, triggering a sense of euphoria[28]. Endocannabinoids also stimulate the production of serotonin, contributing to sustained feelings of happiness and well-being.

Regular workouts in any form help manage mood swings, flush out emotional energy from the body, and keep the energy of the body refreshed.

But exercise can feel like a task, and doing it consistently can feel even more difficult. And this is where most people face the challenge of physical activity. The missing link here is a lack of relationship between body and movement.

Building A Relationship Between Body and Movement

I have joined the gym plenty of times and paid up for a year, thinking this time I will do it regularly. The maximum I have lasted is three months. I got busy, bored or both and gave up. Similar things happened with power yoga and regular yoga. That's when I figured I did not enjoy the workout; I was doing it because I had another goal: lose weight, gain stamina, build endurance, etc.

When I began to dig deeper, I realised that movement in the form of a workout was not a natural part of my routine and life. Also, I never looked at it as an end, but always as a means to an end. My purpose was never the workout, and I was too focused on the result, I never realised how my body felt after the exercise. When the goal began to seem too big or too far away, the motivation to move dropped, and my consistency went down the drain.

It was only when I focussed on how my body felt after a workout that I realised its effects on my body. It made me feel calmer; I particularly enjoyed the slow yoga and the stretches. The feeling of exhaustion and a renewal of energy in the body after a workout was highly satisfying. That's when I started to build a relationship with my body and listened to its need for movement and the form that I and my body enjoyed the most.

Therefore, the first step is to become aware of how you feel after physical activity, what form of activity you enjoy, and how it can become a part of your everyday life. Exercise doesn't have to mean boring. Anything that helps you move, stretch and sweat a bit is a form of exercise. It doesn't necessarily have to be strenuous, structured or repetitive.

Take a few moments and do this:

Close your eyes and take three deep breaths. Tune into your body and become aware of it completely. Tighten your muscles one by one and relax them, getting a sense of muscles in different parts of the body. As you tune in, your body will want to move in a particular fashion - slow, fast, stretching, etc. Become aware of the energy and how it wants to move. If you feel like moving the body in a rigorous manner, look for a rigorous workout style for you. If the body wants to move slowly and stretch or move, look for workout types like yoga, tai chi or something similar. If your body likes to move - walk, jog or run. If your body likes to move in a rhythm, then dance is your thing.

The body's needs can change, so listen to them and do what works best for you. Repetition can kill the joy in movement. Shuffle your style and flow with the energy of the body.

Forms of movement

Yoga

Regular yoga has been helpful in controlling mood swings in the long run. Yoga doesn't mean twisting your body in ungodly ways (at least not for everyone). Yoga literally translates to *yog* meaning union (of *atman and parmatma,* self with cosmos, body with mind and soul).

> "*Several thousand years ago, on the banks of the lake Kantisarovar in the Himalayas, Adiyogi poured his profound knowledge into the legendary Saptarishis or "seven sages". The sages carried this powerful yogic science to different parts of the world, including Asia, the Middle East, Northern Africa and South America. Agastya, the Saptarishi who travelled across the Indian subcontinent, crafted this culture around a core yogic way of life. Patanjali's Yoga Sutras provide the traditional foundation of yoga, in which he outlines an eightfold path of the practice. Known as the 'Eight Limbs of Yoga,' this path offers a guide to individuals who are dedicated to creating a union between body, mind and spirit.*"

Whether you are a sanyasi, yogi or a person of the world, yoga can benefit each one in ways that are beyond physical. A set of simple asanas, deliberate and controlled movements coupled with some breath work can create so much change in the way the mind and body work that you will be amazed. It not only affects the mind but also gives the body a complete workout.

Deep breaths and gentle stretches are like waves washing away worries, leaving you feeling serene and centred. You can train with a yoga therapist to learn the correct way of breathing with the asanas.

Cardiovascular Exercise (commonly known as Cardio training) and Strength Training

Cardiovascular exercise, whether in the form of running, cycling, or dancing, acts as a powerful catharsis, purging the mind of negativity and leaving room for a rejuvenated spirit. As the heart pumps faster, stress and tension are expelled, making way for a flood of clarity and emotional release. Cardio releases endorphins, those feel-good chemicals that put a smile on your face and beat the blues. Aerobics, high-intensity cardio, can be your best friend when looking to beat the anxiety out of the body.

Lifting weights isn't just about biceps; it's about building emotional resilience. Strength training is often associated with sculpting muscles, but it goes beyond it. It helps the muscles build strength and endurance, and it is also a metaphor for overcoming challenges and adversity in life. When you lift weights, if you are aware, you can almost feel your muscles releasing and letting go of all that had been stored there.

Dance therapy

Remember that time you danced like nobody was watching and felt unstoppable? That's the magic of moving to a beat.

Dance is also known as movement therapy. It is energy in motion that brings you joy. And if you can dance with a sense of abandon, it can be deeply therapeutic. Dance brings you in touch with the primal energy in your core. This is the reason why Lord Shiva is famous for his dance and is known as the originator of dance forms. We all have heard of one of his dance forms - Tandava (the dance of destruction).

Simply letting the body move with music the way it wants to move is another powerful way of releasing emotions. This is a part of the Somatic Therapy Exercise for healing trauma. Trauma, stress and emotions live in the mind and body. You focus on physical sensations and move your body in ways that feel most comfortable for you.

> *"Trauma is "when too much happens too soon for the nervous system to process," says Valerie Candela Brower, a licensed professional counsellor. When you have been stuck in a fight, flight or freeze response for so long, it is natural for the body to become numb and not feel all that pain and sensations. Moving helps you unlock that response and lets your body release all that it felt."*

This can include jumping up and down, dancing, jogging, stretching, etc. What's important is you don't choreograph your movement, don't decide, don't think. Get in touch with your body, scan it and let it move in a way that is soothing, healing, comfortable and feels natural.

Walking, Hiking, Trekking

There is nothing more rejuvenating than walking through nature, especially with no goal or destination. It is communion with nature in its purest form, like a spa treatment for the soul. The fresh air, the rustling leaves, the chirping birds – they all sing a symphony of calm that soothes anxiety and uplifts your spirit.

Walk with awareness, become present with your body and the surroundings and notice how this washes your being and clears all the stress. The next time you go for a walk, ditch the headphones and listen to the music of nature. Become present to your breath and let your eyes feast on the natural beauty.

There are many forms of movement that you can choose from besides the ones mentioned above - tai chi, Qigong, sports, cycling, house chores, etc.

Choose an activity you like or have enjoyed in the past that suits your fitness levels and abilities. It is best to find a few that you can enjoy as a part of your life. If you are not used to any regular workout, begin with something light, as it will tone your system and then progress to more strenuous ones. For better results, exercise outdoors. Nature is very healing for the mind, body and soul. Enjoy your walks in nature, it works even better.

So next time, choose to walk instead of driving; take the stairs instead of the elevator and let your body move.

If you feel resistance (mentally) to indulging in physical activity regularly, connect with a coach or a therapist to help you make it easy and enjoyable.

CHAPTER TEN

PHYSICAL TOUCH

"We need 4 hugs a day for survival. We need 8 hugs a day for maintenance. We need 12 hugs a day for growth"
—Virginia Satir, a world-renowned family therapist

When a baby is born, it needs the mother's touch to be soothed. That touch tells it that the world is safe, and all is well. A gentle back rub from your partner or a warm hug from an old friend—regardless of its form, a comforting touch brings a sense of pleasure and well-being.

Newborns thrive with the nurturing touch of their mothers, while romantic bonds are strengthened through physical contact. Research indicates that hugging can notably lower cortisol levels, the stress hormone, in the body. Such is the profound impact of physical touch. Hugging has been shown to reduce the levels of stress hormone cortisol in the body significantly. That's the power of physical touch.

Importance of Physical Touch

Human beings are social animals. Positive interaction brings happiness whereas loneliness feels bad. There's an evolutionary reason behind that.

During humanity's early history, amidst constant threats from warring tribes and hungry predators, safety was found in the solidarity of numbers and in the security of belonging to a tribe. This is the origin of tribal mentality. These days, there is not much need for physical security, but for emotional security, the community provides that. This is because people are still hardwired to connect — emotionally and physically — and your brain rewards you when you do it.

> *"Too often we underestimate the power of a touch, a smile, a kind word, a listening ear, an honest compliment, or the smallest act of caring, all of which have the potential to turn a life around."*
>
> ~ *Leo F. Buscaglia*

Physical Touch means life. It's one of the five senses through which we receive information about the world. It is also one of the largest sense organs (skin has the maximum surface area compared to other sense organs). Our sense of touch has been shown to play a large role in establishing how we feel and act toward another person. Hostility, nurturance, dependence, and affiliation are some of the social messages that can be conveyed through touch[29].

Nonsexual touch triggers the release of oxytocin, the "bonding hormone." This sets off a cascade of feel-good neurotransmitters like dopamine and serotonin while also decreasing stress hormones such as cortisol and norepinephrine. These neurochemical shifts result in increased feelings of happiness and reduced stress. As stress levels diminish, heart rate and blood pressure decrease, depression and anxiety lessen, the immune system receives a boost, and even pain relief can be experienced.

A study found that infants who experience more nurturing touch during their formative years exhibit reduced reactivity to stress and lower levels of anxiety later in life. Another study by Dr. Jan Astrom suggests that giving and receiving hugs yield positive effects. Merely a 10-second hug can elevate levels of feel-good hormones such as oxytocin, decrease stress-inducing chemicals like cortisol, and reduce blood pressure.

Simply put, physical touch promotes mental and physical well-being.

We call emotions "feelings", not "sightings" or "sounds" because there is a direct correlation between emotions and touch.

Research has shown that different touch sensations can affect our social interpretations of the people around us in fascinating ways18.

In one study, researchers at the University of Colorado and Yale had an employee of the experimenters (blind to the study's purpose) accompany participants to a designated testing room on an elevator. While riding up, the employee asked participants to temporarily hold a coffee cup, which had either warm or iced coffee, while the employee filled out some basic forms.

After arriving upstairs, participants were then asked to rate a fictional person on ten traits, including things like honest vs. dishonest, humane vs. ruthless, and so on. Ones who'd held the warm cup tended to rate the target person as "warmer"—more humane, trustworthy, and friendly—than those who held the iced coffee. In other words, physical warmth produced "interpersonal warmth" in these participants.

> "*"The body speaks when we do not have words for what we are feeling."*
> *~ Psychology Today*"

Touch serves as a direct means of conveying emotions. In one study, Dr Dacher Keltner and his colleagues separated two participants using a curtain and then asked one participant to communicate a variety of emotions by touching only the arm of the other participant, who then tried to identify the emotion being conveyed. Interestingly, many emotions were correctly identified by touch alone, suggesting that there is a strong link between emotional communication and touch[30].

Trauma and Touch

Many of us experience trauma at some point in our lives. Trauma isn't necessarily something big; it can also be a small event that left a lasting impact on the psyche.

The human mind is designed to cope with stress, which is a part of our everyday lives. But when stress tips over into trauma, it changes us. Trauma changes the neural chemistry and pathways in the brain. Human beings can exist in either growth or preservation mode (also known as survival mode). When trauma happens, the behavioural responses become all about survival and preservation.

Trauma overwhelms the resources we have for coping, and it often ignites the "fight, flight or freeze" reaction at the time of the event, as well as into the future. For someone who has experienced trauma, a touch can be perceived as a threat to well-being, be painful or even life-threatening, even when in a safe space.

It is important for those who have experienced trauma to become familiar with and befriend the sensations in their bodies. It is imperative for their recovery. They are living in bodies and minds that are hyper-vigilant and always defensive, on guard, for potential threats in the environment.

> "*Being frightened means that you live in a body that is always on guard. Angry people live in angry bodies. The bodies of child abuse victims are tense and defensive until they find a way to relax and feel safe. To change this, people need to become aware of their sensations and the way that their bodies interact with the world around them. Physical self-awareness is the first step in releasing the tyranny of the past...The mind needs to be re-educated to feel physical sensations, and the body needs to be helped to tolerate and enjoy the comforts of touch. Individuals who lack emotional awareness are able, with practice, to connect their physical sensations to psychological events. Then they can slowly reconnect with themselves."*
>
> *— Bessel A. van der Kolk, The Body Keeps the Score: Brain, Mind, and Body in the Healing of Trauma*"

Touch Therapy

Touch is a form of love language, a means of communication and a way to bond with others. Since gentle and pleasant physical touch can be very healing and is known to produce happy hormones in the body, releasing stress, and creating feelings of harmony and happiness, no wonder touch therapies are preferred by many, especially those who are kinaesthetic (those who process information more in the form of physical touch and sensations).

Touch therapy is an umbrella term for a hands-on therapeutic body treatment where the therapist physically touches the client in a specific way. The purpose is to balance the energies of the whole body and stimulate the body's natural healing ability. Touch therapy includes reflexology, Reiki, chiropractic, massage, etc.

Reiki

Reiki is an energy healing technique in which a Reiki practitioner (who has undergone formal training in this healing art) uses gentle hand movements and positions to guide the flow of life force energy (what's known in Reiki as life force energy) through the client's body to reduce stress and promote healing.

The word Reiki originates from Japan where 'Rei' means universal consciousness and 'ki' means life force energy. When Reiki flows through the body, it heals the mind, body and spirit. The Reiki healer acts as the channel between you and the universal energy. This energy passes on to you through the healer and stimulates your body's natural healing abilities.

Reiki unblocks and heals the seven chakras and the energy system and thus heals holistically, creating emotional healing as well[19]. People who have experienced

Reiki report feeling more emotionally stable; they have been able to release the stuck emotions in their energy system. A reiki healing session can feel like a very gentle energy cleanse and can trigger a release that's deeper than imagined.

Reflexology

Reflexology is an alternative system of healing that involves applying pressure to specific points on the feet, hands and different parts of the body with the thumb or finger. At times, certain instruments are also used to apply pressure. It provides pain and stress relief as well as heals physical ailments.

When a person feels stressed or has a disease, the flow of life force energy gets blocked in their body. This causes an imbalance in the body, which, if not treated, can lead to further health problems and illnesses. Reflexology aims to keep the life force energy flowing through the body, keeping it balanced and disease-free.

The underlying theory is that different parts of the body have corresponding points on the hands and feet. Stimulating and applying pressure on these points balances the flow of life force energy to that area of the body and provides relief in pain or an illness. People often experience an emotional healing journey with physical healing.

Just like any other alternative healing system, reflexology works on all levels of the being - physical, mental, emotional and spiritual. We cannot separate a person into any of these systems. Everything is correlated - physical affects mental and emotional and vice versa. In Chinese Medicine and the ancient Indian system of Marma therapy, all organs are related to emotions. As you stimulate the meridian of an organ, it also helps release the emotion stuck in that meridian.

Massage

Who doesn't like a good massage after a tiring day? Did you know that massage can also help release many emotions that have been brewing in the body and mind without finding a release?

For every mental and emotional problem or 'knot', there is very likely to be a corresponding physical 'knot' in the body and vice versa. All emotions and memories are stored in the body, tissues, and muscles. When the spot of the knot is deeply touched through massage, it not only releases the physical pain but also helps release the emotional knot by bringing it to the surface and making it accessible.

During massage sessions, therapists frequently encounter areas of the body that feel tense or tight. These sensations often indicate areas where the client may be holding negative emotions. The tightness in these areas can obstruct the flow of energy within the body, signalling areas that may benefit from focused attention and release.

When a massage therapist begins to work on that area, the emotions begin to release. It is normal for tears to happen when receiving a good massage. Deep tissue massage can lead to major emotional healing. It helps release negative emotions that have been stored in the body for years. Cranio-sacral massage techniques are also helpful in getting negative emotions to release.

At times, there is a deep sense of release accompanied by a lightness as if a weight had been lifted. So, the next time you feel down and low, go for a massage or even a head massage.

Cuddle Therapy

Cuddle therapy is coming up as a form of therapeutic healing, and there are professional cuddle therapists.

Yes, that's true!

For the uninitiated, "cuddlers" are professionals who offer nonsexual cuddle sessions. They provide hugs and snuggles to people and charge them by the hour.

For some individuals, the intimate touch they desire in relationships may be lacking or may manifest in the form of abuse. Cuddle therapy offers a supportive avenue for victims of domestic violence to reintroduce touch into their lives in a safe, healthy, and respectful manner.

This is what a typical cuddle session would look like.

Before any cuddling or touching, the practitioner and the client discuss about their feelings and boundaries. Then, they can choose a comfortable place to cuddle, whether on a sofa, in bed watching a movie, or lying down while listening to music. They can talk or stay in silence as long as it matches the client's needs. However, cuddle therapy encompasses more than just physical contact. Cuddlers also assist clients in setting boundaries, discussing consent, and guiding them in fostering a healthy connection with their bodies.

The power of touch is something most of us can benefit from.

CHAPTER ELEVEN

CREATIVE PURSUITS

"At the deepest level, the creative process and the healing process arise from a single source. When you are an artist, you are a healer; a wordless trust of the same mystery is the foundation of your work and its integrity."
– Rachel Naomi Remen

Creativity is a powerful way of expression and self-discovery. The mere act of engaging in a creative pursuit, be it writing, art, poetry or dance, it touches the depths of our emotions and psyche.

Creativity is an energy that comes from the Sacral chakra and is expressed through the Throat Chakra. When you engage in creative artwork, no matter what it is, it lets the energy flow through the body, through the energy centres and brings a sense of harmony and satisfaction that is unparalleled.

But when creativity is blocked, either because of life becoming busy or some other reason, it also begins to block our body's energy system. And we know when the energy system is blocked, problems begin - physical and emotional.

One of the most significant benefits of engaging in a creative pursuit is the opportunity for emotional release and processing. Creativity comes from the deepest emotions and experiences. Just like in body movement, if you can allow the creative energy to flow and flow with it instead of binding yourself in a form, you will be amazed at the emotional release that follows with it.

By engaging in writing, painting, or dance, you can transform your feelings of joy, sorrow, anger, or confusion into tangible and expressive forms. This cathartic process facilitates emotional healing, enabling individuals to gain a deeper understanding of their inner selves, navigate challenging emotions, and rediscover a sense of clarity and renewal.

How Creativity Helps

When you engage in a creative activity, you enter into a state of mindfulness and meditativeness. When you begin to flow with it, the mind becomes empty of thoughts and conditionings; it enters the alpha state - the meditative state. This results in a reduction in the stress and anxiety levels.

It is beneficial and necessary for those who have blocked expression because of some trauma or who have health issues related to the throat and thyroid. When the expression (the throat chakra) is blocked, it helps to express creatively through forms other than words. This opens up the channels and provides relief and emotional healing.

If you are prone to mood swings and are hyper-sensitive to emotions and feelings, a creative hobby will help you regulate your nervous system and provide you with much-needed relief and soothing.

Mental Health and Creativity

The Mental Health Foundation states that participating in the arts can enable people to deal with a wide range of mental ill-health conditions and psychological distress. Art therapy is widely used in conjunction with other therapeutic interventions to help improve mental and emotional health.

Study after study demonstrates that creative pursuits enhance psychological well-being and can help guard against depression and anxiety. Art therapy allows people to express emotions they can't put into words. Music soothes the soul and reduces stress. Creative writing and journaling give people an outlet to process their journey. Dance provides a mind-body release from tensions.

Art and craft give you a sense of control over an aspect of your life. It builds confidence and resilience and raises self-esteem. Whether you're refining your writing, painting or vocal skills, developing and channelling them into hobbies yields a great sense of pride and purpose.

How to get started

If you are unsure of how to express or uncover your inner artist, here are a few things you can try.

- **Brainstorm ideas** - Find out what inspires you, attracts you and appeals to you. Make a list of creative hobbies that you can pursue like arts, music, dance, writing, photography, design, cooking, theatre etc.

- **Research** - Explore these ideas in the form of books, courses, classes and even online courses to see which one appeals to you
- **Begin small** - Do not over-commit to an extended class or project. Start with a short-term course or a small little project. When you see progress, you will either be inspired to take it up in depth or drop it and move on to something else.
- **Reflect** - Notice how each art form makes you feel. Does it inspire joy and satisfaction in you, or does it feel like another task you are doing that makes you anxious?
- **Explore** - Keep exploring until you find the right fit for you. It is a process of discovery. Yet don't let the process overwhelm you. Make it fun and keep it light-hearted.

Remember, creativity should be playful and energising. So go ahead and indulge in an art form that brings you joy.

CHAPTER TWELVE

ELEMENTAL HEALING

"Fire, Earth, Air, Water -- one or more of these elements may make you restless. You need to spend them properly to find peace. To spend fire, burn outdated structures, taboos and so on. To spend Earth, build a structure, a good habit and so on. Spend air through creativity, spend water through serving and healing people."

— Shunya, Author ofImmortal Talks

We, along with the universe, are made of 5 elements - Earth, Water, Fire, Air and Space. In Indian spirituality, this is known as the Panchmahabhut. These elements make the nature and the laws of the nature. Earth provides our home, a base to live on; we drink water for sustenance; we are 70% water; we cook food on fire, internal fire digests food in the body; we breathe air and oxygen; the universe is the space that holds us.

Emotions are water, thoughts are air, action or behaviour is fire and what is created out of all these is

Earth. Whenever one or more of these elements within us becomes imbalanced, it creates disharmony and disease. If we want to manage and handle emotions, we can take the help of these five elements too.

Let's look at each element and how it can help us regain balance and harmony.

Earth

Earth or Mother Earth is also commonly known as Gaia. She supports us, gives us birth and helps with our sustenance by providing food. Bones and muscles represent the earth element in our body.

An imbalance in the earth element can make you feel spacey, ungrounded or lost. It can happen when we are either too engrossed in the anxieties of the future or lost in the what-ifs of the past. It is essential to come back into the present and be in this moment to balance the earth element.

Ways to balance Earth element

1. Grounding

Grounding is a technique that will help you become more present in the Now. It is about connecting to yourself in this moment and helping you increase your awareness of yourself.

Visualise yourself like a tree, with your roots going deep into the Earth. Keep breathing and see your roots or grounding cords moving further downward through the foundation of the building you are in, into the layers of the ground below you and down into the centre of the planet. The roots anchor into the planet's centre firmly as a tree with roots that wrap around the planet's centre, as a waterfall with a constant unwavering downward flow. Breathe in and allow yourself to feel rooted in the moment.

Release all the pain, stress, worries and negative attitudes out of the body through your grounding roots.

2. Connect with nature

When you walk barefoot on the grass, there is an exchange of current or ions between the body & Earth. This heals your body at the cellular level and provides many health benefits[20]. Walks in nature are very soothing for this very reason.

Hug a tree. A tree is a living entity that breathes. Tree represents a steadiness that we desperately seek amid emotional storms. When you hug a tree, the exchange of ions and positive energy is rejuvenating for the body and mind and provides a release for stuck emotions and fluctuating moods.

Practice gardening. The act of growing plants is a very satisfying activity. When the plant grows and flowers, the body releases the reward chemical - dopamine. Also, you are directly working with Earth, which is a healing substance. Soil is a living entity. Interacting with it is healing for the body and nervous system.

Water

"Aapo va idam sarvam visvaa
bhutaanyaapahpranaa vaa aapah pasava aapo

annamaapoamrtamaapas samraadaapo
viradaapas svaraadaapaschandasyaapo
jyotiisyaapo yajusyaapas satyamaapassarva
devataa apobhur bhuva suuva raapa Om.
–Mahanarayana Upanishad 4.29

The whole universe is made up of water. All beings are made up of water. The vital airs are the effects of water; cows are also the effect of water; food comes from water; nectar, too, comes from water; all the kingdoms, cosmos, Vedic metres, all are made of water; water is truth and all the deities are water; all the worlds are made up of water."

Water is the source of life. We are 70% water. A human can survive without food for extended periods but not without water. It is the most essential element for life, second only to Air. There is no substitute for water.

Spiritually, water is associated with emotions. Emotions are just like water. They rise within us, often unbidden, take no account of reason or thought, and, without awareness, can lead to confusion and imbalance.

When the water element is also thrown out of balance, it can make you over-emotional and unwilling to adapt to change. You may feel water-logged emotionally.

Ways to balance the Water element

1. Water therapies

Water helps to clean your energies as well. Water is a natural cleansing agent for the energies. Showers or dipping your feet in lukewarm water ensures all that negativity you may have picked up during the day gets cleared out, leaving you feeling refreshed and relaxed. Therefore, it is a good thing to do it at the end of the day.

Drink sufficient water. Every function of the body requires water. Sometimes, when emotions feel stuck and unmoving in the body, it can be due to dehydration. So, sufficient water is needed in the body to move the energy of emotions.

Cold showers are an excellent way to balance the water element. It reduces anxiety, improves blood circulation, energises the body and strengthens the immune system. It balances mood and emotions.

Hot water baths with some added sea salt or Epsom salt soothe and relax the nervous system, sending a message to your brain that all is well. As you soak in the water, visualise the body releasing all that negative energy, pain and soreness being sucked out of the body by that warmth and salt. Breathe and relax until comfortable.

2. Crystals and essential oils

Keep Aquamarine crystal near you. It looks like water and helps reduce water retention in the body. Blue Aventurine, Azurite and Chrysocolla are also beneficial for balancing this element. Different crystals help and work with many different emotions. Smokey Quartz helps with grounding and feeling settled; Citrine helps with procrastination; Carnelian helps with creative blocks and guilt; Turquoise helps with fear of expression, etc.

Some essential oils that support emotions are patchouli, ylang-ylang, jasmine, neroli, rose and sandalwood. You can use them in diffusers or directly apply them to the skin.

For skin application, use essential oils that are specifically for that purpose. You can also massage yourself with oils infused with essential oils.

Essential oils like frankincense, geranium, jasmine, melissa, rose and ylang-ylang help with lack of self-worth and feelings of mistrust.

3. Using Charged Water

Water has a very good memory. Its molecular structure holds information in the form of vibrations. Dr. Masaru Emoto has scientifically proven the effect of thoughts, especially on the structure of water. Using charged water for day-to-day activities provides many benefits for a healthy body, mind and soul. You can charge the water in the following ways:

- **Magnets:** Magnetised water is energy-building, activating, cleansing and detoxifying. Magnetised water has been known to cure bladder problems, and menstrual issues, builds natural resistance power and even gives relief in joint pains. Water can be magnetised using strong magnets. They should be kept in contact with glass containing water for 12 to 24 hrs. Such water remains charged for 3-4 days and should be consumed half a glass at a time.
- **Using Life Force Energy:** Those possessing knowledge of healing sciences like Reiki, Pranic Healing or any other sort of healing can charge the water by giving it healing for 3 to 5 minutes.
- **Mantras:** Chanting Mantras produces positive vibrations that charge the water with healing properties. If you have been chanting a mantra regularly, it will

produce a more profound healing effect on the water. One can chant different mantras for different purposes. Some popular mantras are the Mahamrityunjaya Mantra, Narayan Mantra, Gayatri Mantra, Durga Mantra etc.

- **A simple and pure intention** of positivity to cleanse, purify and charge the water also works wonders in case the above methods cannot be used. Our thoughts produce the most powerful vibrations, which affect our body and the environment. Therefore, it is crucial that one should hold only positive and loving thoughts.

Fire

Fire is the transforming element. It transforms anything that comes in contact with it. Within us, fire is in the form of digestive fire that digests and processes food and transforms it into energy.

Our Gut contains 500 million neurons working as a second brain, responsible for a lot more impact on our behaviours than we can imagine. Interestingly, most of the communication is from the Gut to the brain and not vice-versa. Our Gut is processing so much information and is triggering emotions - good and bad. This is why it is also known as the second brain.

Therefore, the fire element affects our moods and emotions in real-time. And the biggest source of fire element in our lives is the Sun. Heat and light influence the internal fire element, changing our metabolism. Remember, the metabolism is not just about food, it is also of thoughts, feelings and situations.

Ways to balance fire element

1. Watch your diet

High levels of anxiety, anger and stress can be correlated to increased fire element. When we are stressed, we keep stuffing our bodies with food to push those feelings down. But the natural wisdom suggests giving your fire a break by fasting. Consume fresh and raw food only. Drink plenty of water and have more liquids in this fast. Balancing your nutrition and diet will help balance the fire within.

2. Sunshine

> "*"Keep your face to the sun and you will never see the shadows."*
> *— Helen Keller*"

Less fire element can lead to depression, sadness and other emotions on the lower end of the vibrational scale. Sunlight is the best antidote for it. For thousands of years, civilisations revolved around daylight, and many religions worshipped the Sun as the source of all life. But our modern life has changed our working and living patterns; we are now majorly dependent on artificial light, which has led to lowered physical and psychological health and overall productivity.

Light has a direct correlation with moods and the body's circadian rhythm (Body clock). Bright lights uplift the mood; dim lights put us in sleepy states. That is why it is advised to have soft and yellow lights in the bedroom. In contrast, study rooms will do better with natural or white light.

Not enough exposure to sunlight can cause SAD (seasonal affective disorder) or, in simple terms, depression with a seasonal pattern. This is why the primary treatment for this kind of depression is light therapy box, which mimics natural sunlight and stimulates the brain to make serotonin.

Early morning rays of the Sun are considered the best for the body. They do not have harmful properties and provide the benefit of sunlight more effectively. There are yoga rituals based on the Sun - Surya Namaskar or the Sun salutation. It is performed facing the east. One can also chant the Surya mantra for additional benefits while performing it.

Soak in the sunlight and its warmth; allow it to raise your vibrations and dispel the blues.

Air

Air is the breath of life. As we breathe the air in and out, we also breathe the Prana energy or the life force energy, which drives us and keeps us alive.

Have you ever noticed your breath change with what you are feeling? When you're relaxed, your breath becomes slower and deeper. Alternately, when you are feeling fear and anxiety, your breath becomes shallow because of the fight, flight or freeze response.

Breath is our connection to the mind and body. It also connects to the energy flowing through our system. When you find yourself in a lowered mood, check your breath. Chances are you may have a shallow breath and will mostly be breathing till your throat.

Your emotions are closely linked with your physical (body) state, including heart rate, blood pressure, and how you breathe. They affect your nervous system and vice versa. This is good because it means you can affect how you feel by influencing your nervous system. A 2017 study[21] suggests that specific nerve cells connect breathing with mental and emotional states.

Medical practitioners, at times, suggest breath-control exercises for people with stress disorders. Similarly, the practice of pranayama — controlling the breath to shift one's consciousness from an aroused or even frantic state to a more meditative one — is a core component of virtually all varieties of yoga.

You can help regulate your nervous system by using breathwork to simulate a more regulated state for your body. One of the fastest ways to do this and thus change your mood is to change your physiology, and you can do that by simply changing how you breathe.

Breathing exercises to try

1. Breathing from the Diaphragm

Breathe deeply down to your stomach. As you breathe in, let the stomach expand, suck it in as you exhale. You can place your one hand on your stomach and the other on your chest to get the hang of it initially.

2. Paced Breathing

Breathe in for a count of 4, hold in for four and exhale for a count of 6. Doing this stimulates the vagus nerve (it connects the brain and body), which helps bring the body into a state of relaxation[22].

3. Meditative breathing

Let yourself breathe naturally without changing the pace. Keep your focus on the breath, feeling the inhalation and exhalation. Gradually notice the breath becoming slower and deeper, keeping your attention on the inhalation and exhalation. Doing this for a couple of minutes helps the body relax and calms the mind.

Practice bringing attention to your breath with simple tasks like filling up your water bottle, waiting at a red light, sipping your coffee or tea, etc. Include this practice in your everyday life.

CHAPTER THIRTEEN

SPIRITUAL - OF THE MIND AND SOUL

In the previous chapters, we explored emotions and moods and their purpose for us. We also explored the physiological ways of managing emotions and moods through lifestyle and the five elements. There is another aspect to emotions and moods as well - it is the cognitive and spiritual aspect.

Modern psychologists believe that thoughts affect feelings, which in turn influences behaviour.

We have addressed the aspect of behaviour influencing thoughts and feelings. Now it's time to explore the aspect of thoughts (mind) influencing emotions and moods.

Why do we need to understand and change our thoughts?

Thoughts are simply perceptions, how we perceive an event or a behaviour. Based on our perception, our mind takes a call on whether it's a threatening situation or not; in other words - is it a survival threat?

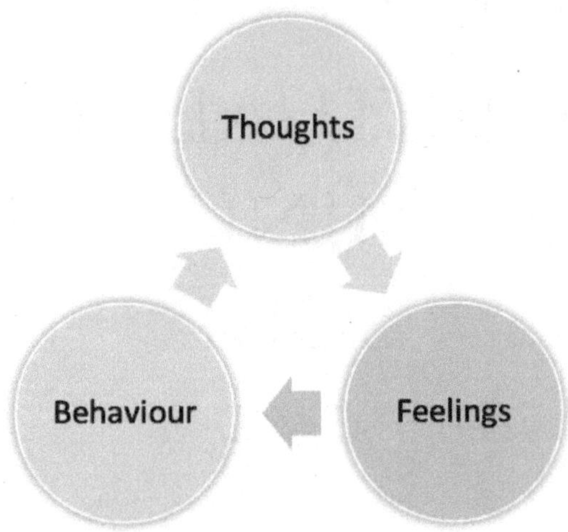

This implies that it is our perceptions which are running the show. But if changing the perceptions was this easy, I wouldn't be writing this, and there would be no need for psychologists, coaches, and therapy. But there are things you can do and understanding that you can cultivate to help yourself shift your perceptions and you will find a change in your emotions and moods.

Role of spirituality

We are not just mind and body. There is also the soul. In Indian spirituality, we talk about dvaita and advaita philosophy. Dvaita, the philosophy of duality, says there are two entities - body and soul. According to this, the world is real. The Advaita philosophy says there is not 2, but one -

the soul. The body is simply a physical manifestation of it or a clothing that the soul adorns when it comes to earth. According to this, the world is an illusion.

But there is no conflict between these two philosophies, although they seem to be opposites of each other. Because the ultimate goal is Oneness, and it is beautifully described in this saying from Isha Upanishad.

> "ॐ पूरणमदः पूरणमदिं पूरणात्पूरणमुदच्यते।
> पूरणस्य पूरणमादाय पूरणमेवावशष्यिते॥
>
> *Om Puurnnam-Adah Puurnnam-Idam Puurnnaat-Puurnnam-Udacyate |*
> *Puurnnasya Puurnnam-Aadaaya Puurnnam-Eva-vashisshyate ||*
>
> *That is whole;*
> *this is whole;*
> *From that whole this whole came;*
> *From that whole, this whole removed,*
> *What remains is whole.*"

This means that if you take away something from the whole, the Absolute (Brahma), the Absolute is still whole, and the thing that's taken out is also whole, even though it's a part of the whole. This is an epic way of describing Oneness.

Bhakti Yog is about the dvaita philosophy where the worshipper and the worshipped are separate. Jnana Yog is about advaita philosophy where the understanding and the goal is of Oneness with the creator. Indian spirituality propounds many ways of reaching enlightenment and becoming one with the divine. Each individual, according to their understanding, can choose a path and follow it.

In the Bhagavad Gita, Lord Krishna talks about both philosophies. He says that there is a soul and body (senses). As long as the soul is driving the vehicle, there is balance. But when the senses take over, you forget that you are soul, and imbalance occurs. But Lord Krishna also says that the only reality is the soul, that is you, not the body. We take birth in a body and leave it when we die. The soul never dies; it is immortal.

Deriving from this concept, body and mind seem to be two separate entities, but in essence, they are one. They are parts of the same being; one affects the other and vice versa. The problems happen when we forget that we are not the body or the mind, we are beyond this.

Therefore, I have also explored the spiritual aspects of managing emotions in this section, which includes meditations, energy care and a spiritual mindset to provide you with all kinds of tools and techniques to help yourself in your everyday life

CHAPTER FOURTEEN

MEDITATION

"I'm simply saying that there is a way to be sane. I'm saying that you can get rid of all this insanity created by the past in you. Just by being a simple witness of your thought processes.

It is simply sitting silently, witnessing the thoughts, passing before you. Just witnessing, not interfering not even judging, because the moment you judge you have lost the pure witness. The moment you say "this is good, this is bad," you have already jumped onto the thought process.

It takes a little time to create a gap between the witness and the mind. Once the gap is there, you are in for a great surprise, that you are not the mind, that you are the witness, a watcher."

– Osho

So much has been said about meditation and its benefits that talking about it seems cliched or almost unneeded. Yet most people think of meditation as an activity where you sit with your eyes closed and do nothing, think nothing.

That is true to an extent, but that is not the only form of meditation and is certainly difficult for beginners or amateurs. Meditation has plenty of benefits, but one of the topmost reasons why people don't do it is because they find it boring or too difficult to practice.

This is why I am talking about it here - busting some myths and bringing forth some truths about Meditation.

Myths and Truths

First, Meditation is not an activity; it is a state. When you use the word meditate, you turn it into a verb, which means it's something to do. But in truth, meditation is not something you do; it is something you become. This is why it is a state to achieve rather than an act to do.

Second, meditation, in itself, doesn't do anything. When you are in a meditative state, plenty of things happen in the body and mind. Your heartbeat and breathing become congruent, brain waves slow down, the body relaxes, and stress hormone lowers. All this sends a signal to the brain that all is safe. As a result, the body begins to heal itself.

Third, there are many forms and various ways of meditation. There is active and passive meditation, chanting or silent meditation, guided or void meditation, and so on. You can be meditative when working, reading, walking or cooking too. Therefore, to think of meditation as sitting silently and thinking nothing as the only way is highly limiting for most individuals.

For the sake of ease of use and understanding here because of common usage by most, I will use the term meditation as something you can do to reach the meditative state.

Background of Meditation

Meditation has evolved from the Ashtanga Yoga. There are seven limbs of Patanjali's Ashtanga yoga. They are:

1. Yama (Principles or moral code)
2. Niyama (Personal Disciplines)
3. Asana (Yoga Positions or Yogic Postures)
4. Pranayama (Yogic Breathing)
5. Pratyahara (Withdrawal of Senses)
6. Dharana (Concentration on Object)
7. Dhyana (Meditation)
8. Samadhi (Salvation) State of Super bliss, Realization of God

Meditation, or Dhyana, is the 7th limb of Patanjali's eight limbs of yoga. 'Dhyana' is derived from the root words 'dhi' and 'yana'. 'Dhi' means to perceive, think or reflect, and 'yana' means path, course, journey or movement. Therefore, Dhyana means a process, path or journey of reflection. Another interesting meaning is the derivation of 'Dhyana' from the root 'Dhyai', which means think, contemplate or meditate, bringing us to a state of meditation[31].

What does meditation really do?

Meditation shifts your brain waves into the alpha state and further into theta and delta. These relax the mind and body. It is also the hypnotic state of mind, which means in this state, it is easy for the mind to change its perceptions, let go of old emotions and make changes to the deeper layers of subconscious conditioning.

Meditation raises your vibrations and releases feel-good chemicals in your body. This uplifts the moods and helps to let go of negative emotions in the energy system. Regular practice of meditation makes it easier for you to relax and think even in times of crisis. It makes you a calmer and more confident individual.

The real purpose of meditation for those living in this world (as opposed to those in sannyasa or asceticism) is to enable you to move through the challenges of everyday life with ease and calm. Daily life is full of stress and can throw up challenges (perceived as survival threats by the mind) at the drop of a hat.

Whenever the mind switches into survival mode, the thinking brain shuts down or diminishes in capacity. This is because the speed of the subconscious (or the survival instincts) is super-fast, which is needed to make decisions in the face of survival threats. The thinking mind or the conscious mind is slow in speed compared to it.

In everyday life, you don't encounter life-threatening situations that often, but the mind perceives the stressful situations also as survival threats and keeps signalling the brain to produce more stress hormones constantly. In this scenario, the mind does not have the space, time and capacity to think if this stress is a survival threat. In other words, it keeps taking the false alarms as true.

Meditation helps to create that space and time for the mind to be able to discern if there really is any need for stress and stress hormones. Hence, meditation creates this gap, this space to think and breathe. Therefore, a person who meditates is less likely to feel stressed unless required and can make informed decisions instead of impulsive actions.

This is how meditation helps with emotional balance and control, deepened self-awareness and spiritual growth.

Ways of Practising Meditation

Meditation is not just about sitting in one place and thinking nothing. In fact, according to Vigyan Bhairav Tantra, there are 112 ways to meditate, and these methods were given by none other than Lord Shiva in a conversation with Goddess Parvati.

> "*Devi, the consort of Lord Shiva, posed profound questions about reality, the universe, and the essence of life, like what's the origin or starting point of everything and what keeps the universe in balance, the central force that takes hold of the cyclical nature of existence, like birth, life, death, and rebirth.*
>
> *Goddess Parvati asks:*
> *O Shiva, what is your reality?*
> *What is this wonder-filled universe?*
> *What constitutes seed?*
> *Who centres the universal wheel?*
> *What is this life beyond form pervading forms?*
> *How may we enter it fully, above space and time, names and descriptions?*
> *Let my doubts be cleared!*
>
> *Shiva responded by revealing the 112 meditation techniques, which are intended to guide the practitioners towards a heightened state of consciousness and self-realization. These techniques, referred to as "Sutras," aren't just methods but pathways to help you gain a deeper*

understanding of the universe."

Here are a few ways to practice meditation:

1. Guided meditations

When you are unsure how to meditate or feel very scattered and find it challenging to be present and still, you can try guided meditations to begin with. Choose a quiet, serene place, preferably a garden or riverside, if you can access it. Or else, a corner in your room will be an excellent place to start with. Play the guided meditation with gentle music and follow the narrator's instructions.

2. Focussing on an object

You can choose any object to focus on - external objects like a peacock feather or flame or an internal object like your breath. Focussing on your breath is perhaps the second most easy way to meditate. Breath is your constant companion, and you don't need anything else. Close your eyes and focus on your breath going in and moving out. You can focus on the starting points of the breath and gradually move on to focusing on the empty spaces between two breaths.

3. Chanting meditation

Chanting meditation involves chanting a mantra or a sound while you meditate. You can choose any mantra or sound per your preference and chant it repeatedly with complete awareness.

4. Mindful meditation

Observe your thoughts moving in and out of your mind. Don't engage with them; don't flow with them; watch them like watching a parade or a movie in a theatre. If you find yourself having moved into a story with the thought, bring yourself back to watching like a spectator. Eventually, the mind begins to become empty.

5. Moving meditation

This is the kind of meditation where you become intensely aware of your actions and movements as you go about doing your work every day. You are not absent; you are not in the past thinking about those good old days or the tragedies, and you are not in the future worrying or daydreaming. You are absolutely present in this moment, present with yourself and your work. This means whatever you do can become a meditation - reading a book, writing a letter, watching something, cooking, travelling, walking, working and so on.

There are plenty of ways to meditate. Find one that works for you, explore different methods and give them a try for some time before deciding. As with each new skill, this is also going to take some time to build and become a part of your being. Give yourself that time and patience for each technique you try.

CHAPTER FIFTEEN

Developing New Perspective

"We see the world not the way it is, but the way we are"
– Talmud

Different people see and perceive the world differently based on who they are and where they come from. When listening to something, chances are that you will focus your attention on what interests you, what is familiar, or what is important to you.

> *"The crisp morning air brought a new routine for a young couple. As they sipped their coffee in their cosy kitchen, the woman's gaze would inevitably drift across the street, landing on their neighbour's laundry line.*
>
> *"Look at that," she'd sigh, pointing to a faded shirt. "She doesn't know how to wash properly. She must be using the wrong detergent."*

Her husband would simply smile and nod. This became a daily ritual, a chorus of disapproval accompanying the flapping laundry. The young woman, convinced to the point that her neighbour needed an intervention, was ready to go over to her neighbour's house and instruct her how to properly do laundry.

One morning, however, she was surprised to see the laundry line, usually a canvas of faded hues, was now vibrant and clean. The woman, speechless, stared at the transformation.

"Did you see that?" she finally gasped, turning to her husband. "She finally learned how to wash! I wonder where she picked up those tips."

The husband chuckled. "Actually," he said, "I got up early today and cleaned our windows.""

It was a simple truth, yet it held a profound weight. All those months, she'd been judging her neighbour through a distorted lens, her own biases colouring her perception. Now, with a clearer view, she realised the laundry had always been fine, just unseen through the grime of her own judgment.

Why is Perspective so Important?

We need to broaden our vision and deepen our understanding of ourselves and the world.

You may ask here, "Why do I need to do that?" The answer is that you don't exist in a vacuum or isolation; you always coexist in a society of people with whom you have a relationship of different kinds, but a relationship nonetheless.

You cannot live in your shells forever. The world around you has a constant influence, sometimes subtle, sometimes not so much. For example, climate change in one part of the world will eventually affect you in some way at some time. Bad roads in your area will affect you in your day-to-day life.

If you do not understand yourself and the people around you in terms of emotions and motivations, life can become a bit like navigating a foggy forest. You stumble around, uncertain of your direction and constantly bumping into unexpected obstacles. As a result, you may experience emotional confusion, poor decision-making, bad relationships, struggles with self-worth, misunderstandings, conflicts, isolation and loneliness.

This is why EQ (Emotional Intelligence) is so important. It helps us understand ourselves, others, and the motivations behind our behaviours and theirs. Perspective is an aspect of EQ that makes all the difference in the world about how you react or respond to a situation.

> "*According to Daniel Schacter, "Perception (from Latin perceptio 'gathering, receiving') is the organization, identification, and interpretation of sensory information in order to represent and understand the presented information or environment."*"

In simple words, perception is when you interpret and make sense of sensory information from your environment. For example, when we see a friend's smile, we interpret it as warmth and happiness; hearing a particular song brings up emotions and memories; smelling freshly baked bread can make us feel comfort and love, etc.

In psychology, perspective is the way you have chosen to see the world. It includes how you see yourself and others around you. It is based on attitudes, beliefs and values about the world, which develop from what you have observed people say and do around you as a child. Everything you see and experience is constantly being organised in the mind based on the factors mentioned earlier. In a sense, your perspective is your filter in the mind.

For example, someone says something mean to you. You could respond to it in many ways.

1. "It's my fault. The other person wouldn't be mean if I did my work properly" — this leads you to feel sad and become more self-critical.
2. "How could they do this? The other person is just trying to put me down and make me look bad." — it might make you feel angry, and you may want to be mean to them, too.
3. "It's not my fault. The other person likes to make people feel bad" — you may just brush off what the other person said and continue with your work and day unaffected.

One situation, three different reactions — all based on how you perceived the event. A reasonably self-assured person will likely respond in the second or third manner, but someone who is insecure and has received criticism a lot is more inclined to react in the first manner.

Here are some more examples of how perspective colours our behaviour and decisions.

- If your family always felt like they were scraping by, often going without necessities or experiencing financial instability, a possible belief for you could be that money is scarce and hard to come by. This belief can lead to hoarding tendencies, anxiety over spending, and difficulty feeling secure even with financial stability in adulthood.

- If you saw your parents fight over money in your house and as a child, you may have believed it was because of money and that money is evil. Such beliefs interfere with charging money that you are worth, saving enough money or being comfortable discussing money matters.

- As a child, if you felt emotionally distant from your parents, lacking affection or consistent support, a possible belief that you may have developed is — I am unlovable or unworthy of affection. This can lead to difficulty receiving love, fear of abandonment, and pushing partners away to avoid vulnerability.

- You go through a traumatic break-up or betrayal of trust in a close relationship, or you witness it. You may begin to believe that Love is fleeting and leads to heartbreak. This can lead to commitment issues, difficulty letting go of past hurts, and fearing getting hurt again.

If any of these or other such beliefs or values about the world are true for you, you are likely to see behaviours and events through the lens of such beliefs and feel and behave accordingly.

This will be true as long as it isn't changed through either an intense experience or active intervention in therapy.

The Link Between Perspective and Emotions

Let's imagine two people who visit a neighbour, and this neighbour has a dog. The neighbour's dog, a bundle of fur and wagging enthusiasm, bounds towards the two visitors. For one, their breath catches in their throat, and they see a predator in disguise, teeth glinting in the sunlight. Shadows of past encounters dance in their mind, turning the playful pup into a snarling beast. For the other, their eyes sparkling with delight, sees a furry friend, a promise of wet noses and joyful barks. Years of shared laughter and muddy paws have painted the dog as a beacon of warmth, and their smile stretches wide in welcome.

Remember the triad of thoughts and emotions.

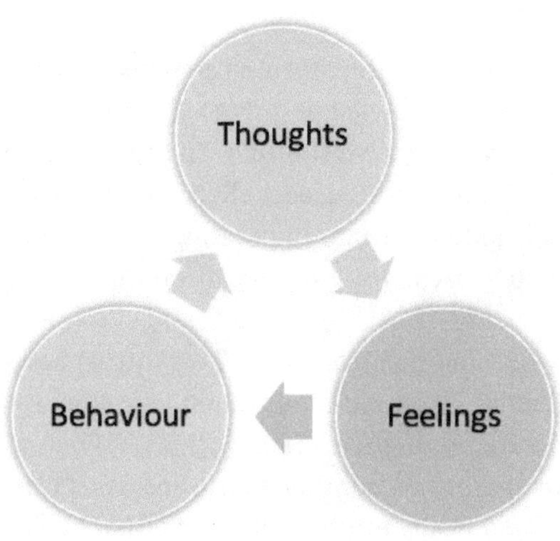

What you see depends on how you look. A situation is seen through the lens of the perspective; it triggers thoughts. Your thoughts trigger a chain reaction of emotions that lead to taking action.

When an initial thought is negative, it can influence your next move. Choosing an action that perpetuates negativity can trap you in a cycle of low moods. The same is true for good moods.

So, whether you know it or not, your perspective is the driving force behind your moods and emotions. This implies that if you shift your perspective about a situation, you can better handle your emotions.

How to Shift the Perspective

1. Awareness

The journey to a transformed perspective begins with a crucial step: acknowledging our subjectivity. We realise that the lens we perceive through isn't the reality itself but a product of our experiences, beliefs, and biases. This isn't a harsh self-judgment but a liberating one. It grants us the power to step back, wipe the fog from our lens, and truly see.

This won't happen overnight. This introspection comes with a practice of gentle observation. We start by noticing our automatic thoughts and reactions. "This makes me angry," we might say, but then pause and ask, "Is it truly the situation itself or my interpretation of it that evokes anger?" By questioning our immediate judgments, we loosen the grip of our limited perspective.

As awareness deepens, we see beyond our own narratives. We actively seek diverse viewpoints, listen with an open heart, and embrace the possibility that "things are" not just as we perceive them. This isn't about abandoning our own truth but about enriching it with the richness of other perspectives.

2. Questioning Assumptions

Imagine looking at a sunset through dirty sunglasses. Everything's hazy, right? That's how our perspective can blur the world. But when you become curious and ask, "What's causing this?" that's when you recognise this blur – realising, "Hey, that's just my lens!"

If you assume that everyone has the same beliefs and opinions as you do, it can make your interactions quite difficult. Good questions can spark curiosity, challenge assumptions and broaden our vision and understanding of ourselves and the world. A simple attitude of curiosity can make all the difference.

Whenever you find yourself feeling the weight of emotions or moods, ask yourself these questions?

- What am I feeling?
- What caused me to feel this?
- Is it something they said or did that made me feel this?
- What meaning did I make out of what was said or done?
- Where did I learn to think or feel this way?
- Who else do I know who thinks/feels this way?
- How do they feel/think about this?

If you get triggered in a situation, ask yourself:

- Is it because of something they said/did?
- Is it because of what I said or did?
- Is it mine or someone else's?

This process is about delving into the "WHY" of it all. But this can also trap you into a self-pity mode if you ask the "why" question from a place of wanting to place blame instead of wanting to understand and heal.

There is a difference between

"Why did this happen to me?"

And

"What is causing me to feel this?"

You want to focus on the reason behind your actions rather than on placing the blame on someone.

So, the next time you feel stuck in a rut or want to see things differently, remember the power of asking questions. It can be the key to unlocking a whole new world of possibilities.

3. Step into someone else's shoes

"The wearer knows where the shoe bites"

If you want to know how someone thinks or feels and why they do what they do, it's a good idea to step into their shoes. It can help you understand the thought process behind their actions.

Plenty of times, we get into conflicts or have misunderstandings with others, even our closest loved ones. Often, the cause is we don't know how they are perceiving a situation and what they are feeling. Putting yourself in their shoes can be incredibly helpful in navigating your relationship with them and interpreting their behaviour. However, This doesn't necessarily always grant you immediate access to their thoughts. So, keep an open mind when doing this.

To do this, you must be willing to look at their perspective; otherwise, this won't work, and you will just hear your own judgments and expectations.

1. Sit in a chair and have an empty chair in front of you.
2. Whatever you need to say to this person (whom you want to understand), say it out loud, imagining them sitting in the chair opposite to you.
3. When you feel complete, stand up and go sit in the chair opposite to you as the other person. When you sit here, you imagine getting inside the body and mind of the other person. Close your eyes, breathe like them, sit like them, mimic their posture. Take a few moments to let the feeling seep in.

4. Notice how they are feeling and perceiving the situation or your behaviour. Keep an open mind free from judgment.
5. When you feel complete, stand up, shake yourself out of that identity and come back to your chair.

This will give you an understanding and some clarity about how the other person feels and thinks and what causes them to behave the way they do.

Additionally, this process can also help you when you are in a situation where you don't know how to behave or react. In such moments, it helps to have a role model who you know handles the situation well. This person could be dead or alive, fictional or real, someone you admire.

All you have to do is imagine stepping inside that person, standing/sitting like them, breathing like them and really feeling what they might feel. Then, act like how they would behave.

For example, if a social situation makes you anxious, imagine how a Queen like Cleopatra or a billionaire would behave and step into their world.

Another example could be when dealing with pets makes you uncomfortable, bring into your mind someone who is very comfortable around pets and pets also like to have fun with them. Imagine stepping into their world and behaving like that.

This is called role modelling and is a powerful way to learn new perspectives and behaviours.

4. Separate Fact from Interpretation

A powerful way to uncover and build a different perspective is to start separating facts from interpretation

- separating what happened from what it meant. A fact is verifiably true. An opinion or interpretation is something you think may be true.

When studying tarot, there is an activity where the student is asked to describe the tarot card twice.

8 of Swords from the Rider Waite Tarot

In the first go, only the card is to be described as it is without any emotional adjectives. For example, in this picture, the blindfolded woman is standing with her hands tied and eight swords stuck in the ground. There is some water on the ground in puddles. There is a building in the background. The sky is grey.

In the second instance, the card is to be described with impressions and meanings. A possible interpretation could be that a woman who seems defeated is tied up and blindfolded, stuck in the centre of eight swords, unable to move, see or do anything. She is wearing a red colour dress. There is a huge castle in the background. It seems as if she is alone and left in this deserted place. The puddles of water seem to represent her emotional state of feeling left out, in pieces and abandoned. The sky is grey, and the evening is setting in, leaving her fate in treacherous hands.

Notice the difference between the two descriptions

One contains only facts about what is there. The other description contains assumptions, feelings, descriptions and meanings. People in different stages of life and diverse emotional states will interpret this card in different ways. One might say she is helpless and needs help; another may say she is stuck in a victim mentality when, in reality, she can help herself. But the fact is that both are interpretations based on the emotional state of the reader or querent.

This is what we are doing with every situation. We are presented with some facts, and we give them a meaning (which could be true or fictitious) based on our perspective. If we learn to separate the facts from the stories we weave around them, many problems will dissipate.

Many problems happen because mountains are built out of molehills. In assuming meanings in a situation, facts are often twisted to fit into the meaning instead of the other way around.

Here are some examples of facts and opinions:

Fact: It is 6 degrees outside

Opinion: It is very cold today

Fact: This dish contains tomatoes, onions, and spices.

Opinion: This is the best dish ever!

Fact: The speed of light is approximately 299,792 kilometres per second.

Opinion: Sunsets are the most beautiful moments of the day.

Understanding the distinction between facts and opinions allows us to communicate more effectively, evaluate information critically, and avoid misunderstandings.

5. Shifting your underlying beliefs

Certain ways of looking at the world, like "Black and White" or "All or nothing" thinking, can interfere with developing a different perspective. Some underlying beliefs like "It is always my fault" or "There is only one truth" can stop you from looking at life differently.

Some examples of such thinking and beliefs are:

"I made a mistake on this test. I must be terrible at everything."

"If I don't get this job, I'll never find another one, and I'll be a failure."

"I feel like I'm not good enough, so I must not be."

"They didn't text me back; they must hate me."

"I should be perfect in everything I do."

Such beliefs and thinking styles can lead to a loss of self-confidence, cause anxiety, stress and depression, damage relationships, create misunderstandings, and prevent you from addressing problems and making necessary changes.

To change it, there must be a desire to make life easier or better. Contemplation and self-awareness can help you begin to see that your thinking may be blocking your progress. This can trigger an exploration into the internal mental landscape and explore what within me is stopping me from looking at things another way.

A therapist can also help you with this exploration and shifts. If your underlying belief is that "It's my fault" and guilt is your constant companion, then letting go of the guilt and the belief will begin to enable you to look at things differently. You can use various therapeutic techniques, EFT or NLP to shift your limiting beliefs.

CHAPTER SIXTEEN

HEALING THE EMOTIONS

"If we never let children go through the full wave of emotions when the emotion hits, there won't be the assurance that it will pass. That is scary."

– Krysten Taprell

The emotions as an energy are meant to flow. Flowing emotions conduct useful information to help you deal with what is happening in your environment. But when they cannot flow out of the energy system, they start to accumulate in it.

These accumulated or stuck emotions begin to create hurdles in the freely flowing energy in the body, eventually producing blocks in other areas of life and the body. But when we let feelings happen, they usually run their natural course.

It is essential to understand that emotions are the language in which the soul communicates with the body. If you truly intend to listen to your emotions, they will guide you on why they are here and how to handle them.

Emotions are Energy in Motion (e-motion). They will also provide you with the necessary energy and momentum to bring about a change.

Letting the emotions flow naturally goes a long way in improving and maintaining emotional well-being. But sometimes, with negative emotions, it can be a scary or difficult experience. This is where the following techniques can help you.

1. Emotional Freedom Technique (EFT)

EFT is a powerful technique to help you deal with your emotions in an easy and non-threatening manner. It helps with difficult emotions without overwhelming the nervous system.

Emotional Freedom Technique (EFT), commonly known as Tapping, is a meridian-based energy therapy developed by Gary Craig. It is a simple technique that helps you release any emotions easily and often provides rapid relief from physical-emotional issues like Trauma, PTSD, Phobias, Grief, Anger, Guilt, Anxiety, Addictive Cravings, Nightmares, Abandonment, Fear of Public Speaking, Fear of Flying, Love Pain, Depression, Pain, Headaches and much more).

Emotional Freedom Technique (EFT) is a unique form of "psychological acupuncture" that combines the ancient Chinese meridian system with modern psychology to relieve psychological stress, emotions and physical pain.

EFT, or Tapping, balances the energy system with a tapping process that stimulates specific meridian endpoints on the face and body. This process sends tiny electrical signals through the energy pathways, clearing them of stuck energies and emotions.

Restoring the balance of the energy system neutralises emotional conflicts at their source, allowing the body and mind to resume their natural healing abilities. EFT is safe, easy to apply, and is non-invasive. With EFT, you can resolve the emotions and traumas and let go of stored issues, allowing health, healing and abundance. It creates a space for healing emotions and promoting life transformations.

EFT is clinically proven, and worldwide, people are using EFT to improve health, relationships, business and finances, job satisfaction, manifesting abundance, improving performance in sports, and getting over their fears, phobias and limiting beliefs. Doctors are using it with their patients, teachers with their students to improve performance and grades, parents with their kids to improve their relationships, etc.

How to use EFT

The process of EFT or tapping is easy to memorise and can be done anywhere. Here are the steps that you can follow along.

1. Identify and Locate the Emotion

The first step is to identify the emotion for which you want to use EFT. You can do this by asking yourself:

- What am I feeling right now?
- Where in the body do I feel this feeling? What kind of a sensation is it?

2. Test the Initial Intensity

Measure the intensity of the feeling/emotion from one to ten, where ten is very intense, and one is not at all.

3. The Setup

The Setup is a process we use to start each round of tapping. Start tapping with your fingertips on the side of the hand, called the karate chop, and say the following three times.

"Even though I feel this ________________(name the emotion, where it is located and intensity), I love and accept myself". — 3 times.

For example,

Even though I feel anxious because I am running late, I feel it in my chest; it's a 10/10; I love and accept myself.

Or

Even though I feel angry, I feel it in my jaw; it's an 8/10; I love and accept myself.

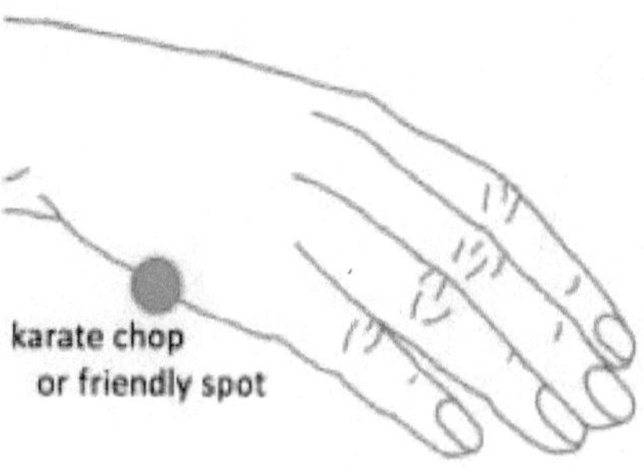

4. The Sequence

Repeat key phrases out loud from the problem, for example, the emotion or the issue, while tapping seven times on the points shown below.

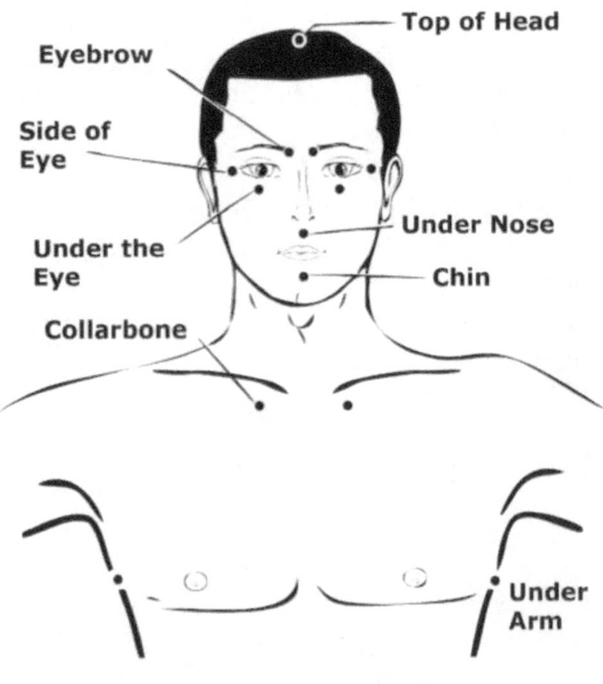

Tapping Points

- EyebrowSide of eye
- Under eye
- Under nose
- Chin
- Collarbone
- Under arm
- Top of the Head

5. Final clearing

Close the process by tapping on the Karate Chop point and saying the starting set-up phrase again one time.

"Even though I feel this ______________(name the emotion, where it is located and intensity), I deeply and completely accept myself". — 1 time.

6. Relax and Breathe

Relax, take a deep breath and take a sip of water. Keep yourself well hydrated during the process so that the toxins that are released can be easily flushed out.

7. Test the Intensity Again

Measure the intensity of the feeling again on a scale of 1 to 10.

You compare this with the previous level to see how much progress you have made. If you are not down to zero then repeat the process until you either achieve zero or plateau at some level.

It is important to measure the intensity as it exists NOW....as you think about it, not as you think it would be in the actual situation.

You can use EFT on yourself as part of a daily program for issues and emotions that you may be facing or that come up during the day, such as anger, anxiety, sadness, etc. or physical pain and tension.

EFT can help you explore deeper core issues affecting your life every day, like repeating patterns, self-sabotage, negative beliefs, etc., and help you on your healing journey. A trained and certified EFT practitioner can help you deal with emotional issues along with physical pain, cravings and other problems as well.

2. Sitting with the Emotions

The more you resist, the more it persists.

That's the rule with emotions too. They are meant to flow, but if you keep resisting them, you block their flow, and they persist in the body, trying to show up, looking for a release. Therefore, the other technique to help the emotions to flow is just to sit with them.

This might seem difficult and even counter-intuitive. But it's a powerful technique that helps you change your perspective of emotions from enemies to messengers.

Every time an emotion arises, it has risen from certain thoughts. The more it grows, the more thoughts it gathers as fuel. You can look at it as a bonfire - It starts with the wood. The wood ignites, and the fire rises. The fire needs more wood to sustain itself. But if you stop adding the wood, the fire will die out and extinguish naturally after a certain period.

The fire is the emotion, and the wood is the thoughts or the story the mind weaves around those emotions. If you can watch the emotion arise, sit through it and focus on the sensations of the emotion in the body without entertaining the thoughts and the story the mind is trying to weave about it, the emotion will naturally ebb away like a tide.

Since emotions are a powerful energy, this exercise can often be challenging to practice in the middle of a strong emotion. Begin this practice for easier or lighter emotions, perhaps even with positive emotions. Once you are well-versed in the process, you will be able to do it for the more negative and stronger emotions as well.

Follow the process:

1. As the emotion arises, sit in a place where you can be present with yourself with little distractions.
2. Notice the emotion that arises, and pay attention to the feelings and sensations in the body that come along with the emotion.
3. Remember to just observe like a spectator. If you are tempted to participate in the emotion, bring yourself back gently.
4. You might notice some stories or thoughts that begin to rise, thoughts about why this happened, the situation, the drama, the movie. They will be extremely tempting but don't flow with them. Observe them like watching a movie in a theatre or on your mobile. Let them come and let them leave.
5. Eventually, as you keep focussing on the sensations in the body, just watching them, the feelings will begin to slowly ebb away.

6. The emotion will feel like it's draining away, losing its power over you.

Throughout the process, keep breathing at a natural pace. Your breath will be your anchor. Anytime you notice your breath changing its pace, bring your focus back to the body.

This process is not about becoming emotionless, but allowing you to feel completely that is safe and harmonising.

CHAPTER SEVENTEEN

ENERGY CARE FOR EMOTIONS AND MOODS

"If emotions and thoughts can impact the structure of water and food, imagine what they do to you on a cellular level in your body?"

— Lisa Manyon, Spiritual Sugar: The Divine Ingredients to Heal Yourself With Love

Emotions and moods are energies and collective energies in motion, respectively. To deal with and heal them, we also need to look at the energy aspect of the emotions. In the previous section, we learned how to deal with emotions by tapping on the body and tapping into emotions to harmonise them. This section will explore the energy aspect of emotions - the imbalance, absorbing emotions and releasing the energy.

There is a small percentage of the population (20-30%) that is HSP (Highly Sensitive Person). Out of these, a proportion of the population is also empaths. Managing emotions is perhaps the biggest challenge for them.

Empaths and Highly Sensitive Person

A Highly Sensitive Person (HSP) is someone with a sensitive nervous system, is acutely aware of the subtle cues in the surroundings and gets easily overwhelmed with external and internal stimuli — pain, hunger, light, sounds. According to Dr. Elaine Aron, HSPs have a complex inner life, they process everything around them much more—reflect on it, elaborate on it, make associations.

Empaths are deeply sensitive people who are highly perceptive and can easily feel other's emotions and energies. The experience goes even further for them as they can experience others' feelings and pain as their own. The term empath is used to describe a person who experiences a great deal of empathy, often to the point of taking on the pain of others at their own expense.

The enhanced sensitivity makes you creative, artistic, altruistic and insightful. But quite often, sensitive people are ridiculed and somehow seen as weak and vulnerable.

> "*Dr. Judith Orloff, author of The Empath's Survival Guide, offers this short quiz to evaluate whether or not you are an empath:*
>
> *Ask yourself:*
>
> 1. *Have I been labelled as "too emotional" or overly sensitive?*
> 2. *If a friend is distraught, do I start feeling it too?*

3. *Are my feelings easily hurt?*
4. *Am I emotionally drained by crowds, require time alone to revive?*
5. *Do my nerves get frayed by noise, smells, or excessive talk?*
6. *Do I prefer taking my own car places so that I can leave when I please?*
7. *Do I overeat to cope with emotional stress?*
8. *Am I afraid of becoming engulfed by intimate relationships?*

According to Dr. Orloff, "If you answer 'yes' to 1-3 of these questions, you're at least part empath. Responding 'yes' to more than 3 indicates that you've found your emotional type." "

As a sensitive person, you experience the world intensely. Even a book, news article or piece of fiction can affect you and make you feel exactly what the protagonists or the characters are feeling. You can sense the energy around you much more easily. When you interact with someone, the subtle shifts in their energy and micro-movements are enough to let you know what is going on for them.

You are also highly attuned to what others are feeling. As a result, you may absorb and take on emotions that are not necessarily yours. So, that unexpected pain or heaviness in the arm could very likely have been absorbed from someone you encountered.

You also feel intensely, and subtle behaviour cues can make you feel plenty of emotions and feelings. Sometimes, these are so subtle that you may not even realise it until it has become a cascade of negative moods.

Before we move on to understanding how to handle emotions, if you are a sensitive person, you need to know this.

The Gift of Sensitivity

- It's okay to be a sensitive person or an empath. It's not a disease or a problem. It's how you experience the world.
- Most of the artists and creative people are highly sensitive empaths. It gives you the ability to experience life in its full colours.
- You find happiness and calmness in the simplest of things.
- Being too sensitive, you can easily gauge the environment and read the subtle undertones of conflict or comfort. It is not easy to lie to empaths; especially if they have accepted their empathic abilities and are comfortable with it.
- You can easily understand and feel what others are feeling, that is why people love to talk to empaths because they are good listeners.
- You experience energies before others can.
- You have an evolved and sharp intuitive sense.
- You tend to absorb other's pain and feelings. This makes you a good healer if you can learn how to handle your empathy and clear your energies regularly. Most healers are empaths. They can sense and even feel the pain of their clients — both physical and emotional. It makes them extremely intuitive and capable as healers because they can get to the root cause of the problem much sooner.

- You can easily adapt to your environment. Empaths are like chameleons. It is their defence mechanism, but when used well, it makes them extremely adaptable.
- Because you feel too much, your capacity for love is also magnified. It helps you understand the needs of your partner and also enables you to love truly and completely.

The Challenges of Sensitivity

Being sensitive to energies will mean that you can easily catch on to the good as well as bad vibes. This creates particular challenges for sensitives and empaths as well. Some of the challenges faced are:

- Sensitivity to the external environment — sights, sounds, smells — can easily cause a sensory overload for you causing you to withdraw from social situations.
- You can easily pick up other's emotions as a sponge and experience them as your own. As a result, someone's sadness or joy will be experienced as your sadness.
- Crowded places can feel overwhelming for empaths. So going to social gatherings and parties can be stressful rather than enjoyable for you.
- Many healers are empaths. This can lead you to absorb your client's pains and problems which, if you are not careful, can cause pain and health conditions for you as an empath.
- Empaths can change their tone of voice, conversation style, body posture and even general outlook to make others feel at ease. Because it feels so natural, you can do it so often and so unconsciously (it is their defence

mechanism), you tend to forget or lose touch with who you are and what you are like.

- You avoid confrontation because doing or saying something that may cause someone to feel angry or sad is extremely uncomfortable for empaths.
- As an empath and a sensitive person, you tend not to have healthy boundaries because it becomes difficult for you to understand where the other ends and where you begin.

This can cause you to feel drained, overwhelmed and exhausted easily. Also, it takes time for you to recharge your energies or unwind at the end of the day.

Techniques to Help with Energies

Whether you are an empath, HSP or none of these, emotions are a powerful force that needs to be understood and managed. There are some techniques and hacks that you can use to protect yourself from energy drain and emotional overwhelm.

1. Create and Protect your Energetic Boundaries

The biggest struggle for Highly sensitive people and empaths is a lack of boundaries. Because there is an acute lack of understanding about sensitivity and empathy, such people usually suffer from sensory overload and emotional overwhelm without any respite.

They usually do not understand healthy boundaries, where they begin, and what their space is. It is essential to understand your energetic boundaries so that you don't unknowingly pick up energies from others.

A healthy aura acts as a natural boundary and a natural protection against negative energies. Aura is an electromagnetic force field around you. It is your energy field that extends all around you - front, back, sides, above and below. It is like an egg-shaped bubble around you at a distance of one arm's length.

It is simple to understand an aura. For example, even if you are sitting with your eyes closed, you would still come to know when someone sits or stands very near you. This happens because that person has entered your aura, which creates an energetic disturbance, and hence, their presence becomes known to you.

If you feel overwhelmed talking to emotionally negative people or if you are the sort of person whom people turn to when they want to share their sorrows, then a strong aura will protect you from their negative emotions and bad moods from affecting you. Also, when people around you are jealous or have harmful intentions, they may unknowingly send you negativity in the form of psychic daggers or knives, which can cause physical or mental trauma. A strong aura is your best protection in such cases.

Defining and repairing the aura

Fortunately, defining your aura through awareness and repairing it is a simple process of visualisation. The underlying premise is that energy follows thought. Wherever your thought goes, the energy will flow there in the way your thought is flowing.

The process of defining your aura is as given below:

1. Close your eyes and take three deep breaths.
2. Imagine or visualise a large egg-shaped bubble surrounding you (from top to bottom and all four sides).
3. Light up the edges of this bubble with a very bright neon colour of your choice. (This defines the boundaries of your aura clearly)
4. Stay with this visualisation, focusing on the shape, size and colour of and within the aura.

To repair the aura

If you notice any tears, holes or breaks in the aura and its boundaries, this indicates the aura is not healthy. Also, if it is lopsided or weak in places, this shows the weaknesses in the aura.

To repair it,

- Visualise the aura as completely healed,
- the holes are filled up,
- the tears and breaks are repaired,
- the size is restored to its normal shape (egg-shaped and equidistant from all sides).
- Maintain this visualisation for as long as possible and repeat it often. This begins to repair the aura (your natural boundary) and strengthen it in the process.

2. Prevent Energy Drain

In our everyday life, whenever we interact with anyone in any way, energetic cords are formed between them and us, whether the interaction is physical or over the phone and Internet. These cords are a means of exchanging energy between two people.

This cord shares energy and transmits a high frequency of communication, which may explain why we often feel and connect telepathically with our partner's thoughts and emotions. Cords can also form between you and a substance in the case of addictions or between your energy and the energy of a past life or present challenging situation.

There are two types of cords. Positive connections that have unconditional love, affection, good times, lessons learned together, fondness, etc. We can never sever the positive cord because it contains all that is good about that relationship.

Negative cords are the negative structures that contain all the negative energies that are present in a relationship, for example, hurt, being cheated on, anger, insecurities regarding that relationship or person, etc.

When you cut cords with someone, it does not mean you will lose contact with the person or weaken the positive connection. On the contrary, cord-cutting clears up space to create a stronger positive connection (if that is what you want).

Attachments form to your energy when fear or judgment arise, enabling the exchange of toxic and dense energy between you and the source of the negative emotion.

These attachments, known as cords, arise from imbalances in your relationships with people or situations. They persist until severed, with some individuals carrying past life cords energetically for lifetimes.

You can form cords with almost anyone that you are connected to. The strongest cords are usually with parents, spouses, lovers, siblings and children. Smaller cords may be formed with bosses, colleagues, teachers, classmates, and acquaintances.

If you feel drained and exhausted after interacting with someone physically or over the phone or the Internet, you may have negative energy cords attached to them. If you have a problematic association or interaction with someone and you are strongly connected to them on an emotional level, cord-cutting can help you immensely by clearing the negative energy and creating space for better communication.

Some Reasons You Should Cut Cords Energetically

1. Completely End a Relationship

When a relationship ends, this is an important step to complete. Cutting cords for this purpose allows you to finally end this relationship and receive a sort of closure, so you can start fresh in the next relationship! It is like turning a new chapter in a book!

2. Disassociating with Lower Vibrations

When you cut cords, this allows for one not to get trapped in the loop of lower vibrations. This happens when one keeps going into similar relationships or towards people that enable negative patterns or emotions. It happens to many people as they say they are going to leave their relationship, but they continue to go back and forth. They are caught in a low vibrational spiral and cannot separate from each other.

3. Repeating the Same Lesson

When a cord is still attached energetically, a person can repeat the same lesson or pattern repeatedly as they are resonating on the same frequency as that old cord. For example, a person who gets out of one toxic or unhealthy relationship and becomes involved in another unhealthy relationship. This is not destiny, chance or bad luck; this is the old cords that are creating and seeking similar connections. The old pattern is still active.

4. Releasing Karmic Ties

Often, we meet the same people from past lives to resolve karmic ties. These connections are in place so that we can learn some lessons. When we cut cords with them and understand the lessons that need to be learned, the issue will finally be resolved in this lifetime.

The Process to Cut Your Cords

There are many ways to cut cords. Here is one of the many techniques for doing this. The most important thing here is that you are ready to do this process and are open to learning the associated lessons from it.

1. Sit with your eyes closed and take three deep breaths.
2. Call in your mentor/guru whose wisdom you trust.
3. Imagine a campfire that is made of unconditional love. Imagine the person with whom you want to cut the cords in front of you.

4. Notice, imagine or visualise any cords or strings attached to this person from your body. You may feel as if you are "making it up" or "imagining" the cords. Allow yourself to trust what you get. Become aware of the cords and the circumstances or emotions surrounding it. (You can ask your mentor)
5. Take an imaginary knife, sword or scissors, cut each cord from both ends and throw the cords in the fire of unconditional love. (You can do this part with the help of your mentor.)
6. Visualise filling up the places where the cord was attached with a green healing balm.
7. Repeat this process until you find there is no cord left. Notice how you feel in the body now and how you feel about the person with whom you cut the cords.
8. Thank the mentor and open your eyes gently.

Doing this process every day will prevent you from absorbing the emotions from someone else, feeling drained and will leave you feeling cleansed energetically.

3. Clearing the stuck energy of emotions

Whether you are an empath or not, your aura constantly interacts with the energies of those around you and picks up their stuff. Empaths happen to absorb more than the others. When you absorb others' energies, you take in their emotions, feelings, thoughts, judgments and opinions.

It is like keeping alien stuff with you, things that are not yours, and it is always a good idea to let them go. Consider it like you go on a beach vacation and you pick all the knick-knacks from every shop, shells from the beach, scarves from the shacks, beer bottle caps, shiny stones, sand particles that get stuck to you and get inside your backpack, etc. All this stuff stays with you in your backpack or bag, even when you return from the vacation. You are still carrying it around. How would that feel?

This is what carrying other's energies within your aura and energy system feels like. It is not yours; it's heavy, takes up a lot of space, and can become bothersome if carried for too long.

Situations when you may want to cleanse your aura and energies are:

- You feel physically drained or lethargic
- You are feeling negative or emotionally low
- When you're experiencing a chronic illness or body aches
- You have been around "negative" or stressful people or in a place that felt negative
- You are preparing for a sacred ritual

Here are a few ways to cleanse your energy system, refresh your energies, and feel uplifted.

1. Salt Water Cleanse

Water and salt have long been considered energetically cleansing substances. Salt can absorb any pain or negativity just as it absorbs water. Water is regarded as a magical and powerful element. You don't have to be spiritual to realise that you feel rested and relaxed after a nice bath or shower.

Water is not only cleansing physically but also energetically. It can absorb and hold energy and easily be programmed (as proven by Dr. Masaru Emoto) according to the vibrations you want or intend. When we use water with the intent of cleaning our aura by sweeping away negative energy, the water absorbs that debris and cleans it away from our energy system.

Salt has the ability to break apart and absorb negative energies. In many spiritual traditions and rituals, salt is used to protect the space energetically by sprinkling it around the ritual space or in the doorways to keep out any negative energy. Just because there aren't enough scientific studies about this doesn't mean it's untrue and should be rejected. There is wisdom in the way of the ancients if only we are willing to look at it from a non-judgmental space.

The salt that you want to use for this purpose is the salt in its crystal form. It can be the sea salt or the pink Himalayan salt known as the "rock salt". They have many more minerals than the common table salt which has been processed. Epsom salts are also known for their pain-relieving properties. But if they are not available easily, you can use the table salt too.

An important thing to note here is to have a clear intention of what you want from the saltwater soaks. Have an intent of releasing all the stuck negative energies from your body and aura into the water. You can focus on observing the energies leaving your body. If you don't want to do that or are too tired, you can relax with your eyes closed and meditate or perhaps read a nice book. Avoid mobiles or any disturbing distractions when doing this process for maximum benefit.

Here are a few ways to use salt water cleanse:

1. Salt water soak

Fill a bathtub with warm water, add in a few handfuls of the salt and soak in it for about 20-30 minutes. You can also add essential oils to this to enhance the benefits. Use lavender to de-stress, eucalyptus to open the channels or lemon grass to feel refreshed.

2. Salt water foot soak

Add a cup of salt to a bucket of warm water and soak your feet in it for 15-20 minutes. This will help release the stress and negativity and help relieve physical pain, too. Remember to flush out this water after use.

3. Salt rub

If you like showers or don't have the means or energy for a soak, then this method is for you. Take some salt in your wet hands and gently rub it on your body. Remember not to scratch your body and avoid any sensitive areas and face. You can even use the salt in a washcloth and rub it on your body. Then, get under the shower and wash away all the energetic debris with the salt and water.

4. Saltwater bowls

If you are prone to overthinking and nightmares or are going through too many negative thought cycles and moods, keep a bowl of salt water on your bedside while you sleep and drain it in the morning. Doing it every night will help with calming the negative thoughts. You can also keep the salt water bowls around the house, especially where negative energy tends to get stuck.

2. Energy Healing

We are energy beings made up of energy, and we run on energy called the life force energy or Prana. Emotions are also energies (e-motion). When they are not allowed to flow, they get stuck in the energy system. Energy healing is a way to have the life force energy flow through the energy system and release any energy blocks.

If you are trained in any healing modality like Reiki, Healing Touch and Therapeutic Touch, chakra balancing, crystal therapy, etc., you can use them to heal your energy system and clear it of any stuck energy. For example, in Reiki, you invite the life force energy or "ki" to flow through the energy system and raise the vibration of the energy in the body. This dissipates all the energy blocks and brings up any residual emotions to the surface to be cleared and released.

Here are some energy techniques derived from various energy modalities that can be easily used by anyone, even those who are not trained in any system.

1. Channelling Emotions

When you express your emotions, you rely on others to handle, respond and honour them. When you repress it, you hand it to the unconscious to deal with it. However, none of these ways are healthy ways of releasing your emotions.

We have dealt with many ways of working with emotions. Here is another method that has its roots in energy work and meditation. Since emotions are energy and they contain information for you to use and work on, an excellent way to deal with the emotional energy is to bring it into awareness and release it. Below is the process that you can use whenever you feel an emotion.

1. As you feel the emotion, take a few deep breaths and allow yourself to come into the present.
2. Ground yourself by visualizing roots growing from your feet and going down into the earth to its core.
3. As you notice the emotion arising in your body, bring it to fullness. Do not use the energy of the emotion to act or create a story. Just stay completely present with the raw emotion.
4. Become aware of the location in your body where you are feeling this emotion. (If you are new to this, it might take a few moments to connect to the body. Have patience, and if unsure, take a guess)
5. In your mind, begin to describe this emotion and the associated feelings in the body in images and words. Describe it in as many details as possible.

    a. What would be a colour for the emotion?
    b. Does it move? If yes, how does it move?
    c. Is it big or small?
    d. Is it intense or mild? Acute or Dull?
    e. What does it look like?

6. As you become more present with the emotion and its descriptions, allow it to fill your body and aura.
7. Now breathe it out into your aura.
8. For a few moments, study this energy. Listen to it. Your emotions may require you to speak, scream, cry or make a movement. Do it. Keep listening. (If it gets overwhelming, gently massage your thymus area and tap under your collarbone.)

    a. You may ask the emotion why it's here.

   b. If another emotion emerges from this, do the same with it. Give it a colour and movement. Listen to it.

9. After a few minutes, thank the emotions and your subconscious for communicating with you and allow these emotions to move out of your body through your grounding cords.
10. Take a deep breath and relax.

Since emotions have a very short life span, doing this begins to give you more control over your reactions when an emotion arises and brings you the gift of information that a particular emotion is carrying.

Remember to reach out for professional help from a therapist or someone trained in handling emotions if this feels like an overwhelming process.

2. Breathe it out

A simpler version of the above process is to breathe out the emotion. For emotions that are not strong enough, like a bit of frustration or sadness, or anything less than a four on a scale of 10, this method can take care of it.

- Bring the emotion into consciousness.
- Imagine it like a balloon or a ball of energy inside you.
- When it's all gathered up, gently blow it out of your mouth.

What really makes a difference is wanting to let go of the emotion instead of keeping it. Plenty of people make the mistake of not wanting to let go of the emotion because they feel if they let it go, they might end up making the same mistake again or end up getting hurt again. But emotion doesn't protect you from that; rather, it prevents you from learning from what happened and moving on stronger.

3. Music and Sound

Music has this unique quality to evoke emotions within you and shift your mood. Sound is a powerful form of energy, and it can help you release any energy that is stuck.

Have you ever cried listening to a song? Or felt nostalgic?

Remember the time when you had a breakup, and you listened to that sad song on repeat?

The music of that song felt like a balm on the aching heart.

It sounds counterintuitive. How can a sad song make you feel better? But the truth is that the sad song was helping you release the sadness within you; it was acting like a catalyst to help you let go of all those negative feelings that were inside you.

Studies reveal that low-frequency sounds are relaxing for the brain, whereas high-frequency sounds improve focus and boost mood. This is why you will find plenty of frequency-based music online to help you sleep, relax or focus.

The benefits of sound therapy aren't widely published in medical journals, but a study in the Journal of Evidence-Based Complementary and Alternative Medicine showed sound meditation can help reduce tension, anger, fatigue, anxiety and depression, while a University of Toronto clinical study showed low-frequency sound stimulation improved sleep and decreased pain in people with fibromyalgia[32].

Sound affects our emotional as well as physical body. Since sound is energy, it easily penetrates the energy system and helps release the energy and emotions that have been stuck.

So, the next time you want to shift an emotion or a mood, use the power of sound therapy. Put on the music that resonates with your desired mood, play an instrument or hum a tune. You can also connect with sound therapists to help you with emotional and physical problems.

4. Hug a tree

Trees and plants are living beings and are storehouses of positive energy. They provide many benefits for humans, like clean air, shade, food, medicines, etc. Spending time in nature has been shown to lower stress, heart rate and blood pressure. It also provides a connection with nature that is healing for the mind and body.

In the late 1960s, Zen Buddhist Teacher Thich Nhat Hanh invented a hugging meditation practice as a Zen practice of interconnectedness and inter-being. He suggested that when hugging is done not just for appearances but with all of mind, body and soul, with complete presence and consciousness, it nourishes the other person and brings healing and happiness.

Benefits of hugging a tree:

- It helps you relax

- It increases the level of oxytocin (bonding hormone) which makes you calm
- It reduces the level of cortisol (stress hormone) in the body helping you de-stress and improve your mood
- It improves your immune system
- It helps you connect with nature and feels very grounding

We all know touch and hugs are vital for emotional and psychological well-being. However, some people are uncomfortable with it because of specific reasons like trauma and abuse. Hugging a tree is easier for them, and it provides similar benefits to hugging a person.

Hugging a tree can be a powerful experience as trees give us unconditionally and never demand anything. Hugging a tree will ground you in an instant and make you feel loved. It will also cleanse your aura.

To hug a tree, stand or sit in front of it, wrap your arms around it, and hold on for a few minutes. You can close your eyes, breathe and become completely present with the energy of the tree.

It is important to do this with a sense of gratitude and respect. Choose a healthy tree that you feel comfortable with and avoid damaging the environment in any way.

CHAPTER EIGHTEEN

AFFIRMATIONS

"Words are energy and cast spells — that's why it's called spelling"
— Bruce Lee

Did you know that your body is listening to everything you are thinking? Words have a lot of power. It is words that can uplift you or tear you down, create possibilities or close them down, build relationships or damage them.

How often have you wanted a few words of appreciation from your parent, teacher, or authority figure? Notice how it feels when you receive words that acknowledge you or your work, and notice how it feels when you don't receive them.

Affirmations use this powerful tool of words spoken to yourself to change the way you think and feel about yourself. They are a way to replace the negative self-talk.

Affirmations are simple yet potent statements that we repeat to ourselves to cultivate positive thinking, boost self-esteem, and reshape our mindset. While they may seem like mere words at first glance, their impact runs deep, penetrating the subconscious mind and influencing our beliefs, behaviours, and emotional responses.

Affirmations can be any positive statements that resonate with you. They can be said aloud or silently to yourself. The statements of affirmations can be used to enhance self-esteem, replace negative self-talk with positive statements, help perform under stress and lead to behaviour change.

> "*Remember, you have been criticizing yourself for years and it hasn't worked. Try approving of yourself and see what happens.*
> *— Louise Hay, You Can Heal Your Life*"

How do Affirmations work?

Your mind and body are always listening to you. Your subconscious mind is very literal — it interprets every word very literally. The words you use - spoken or thought - are creating your reality. If you understand this, you will become extremely careful of anything you think or say.

Unconsciously, it is your words that sabotage your success when you use language that undermines your confidence, focuses on problems and dents away at your self-esteem. "It's impossible to...", "I am not good enough for...", "I had no choice..." etc. These are all statements where you unintentionally give up your power and limit your future.

Affirmations look like wishful thinking, but look at it this way: You perform repetitive exercise to improve your physical health. Similarly, positive words and statements spoken repeatedly can affect your mental health.

Research studies show that spending just a few minutes thinking about your best qualities before a high-pressure meeting or a performance review, for example, can calm your nerves, increase your confidence, and improve your chances of a successful outcome.

Something that's repeated over and over tends to make a dent in the patterns in the subconscious mind. They shift your focus from negative to positive. When the mind begins to see the positive outcome, the opportunities and possibilities open up that can then be utilised.

Why do affirmations not work sometimes?

Many people who have dabbled with affirmations (the keyword being 'dabbled', not the serious practitioners) have often complained that the affirmations they are doing are not working or kept repeating them, but nothing happened.

To understand why this happens, let's take a quick peek behind the curtain of the brain and see what happens in the mind.

The conscious mind is the recording mind — it records information it absorbs from the environment through the senses.

The subconscious mind is the record player — it plays back to you what was recorded. That's it!

Behaviours, perceptions, thought processes, involuntary actions like making the heartbeat, etc., and helping you survive in stressful or threatening situations — these are the tasks of the subconscious mind, and it is doing it beautifully according to what it was taught and what it imbibed.

Now the question arises: why is it not imbibing the affirmations you are speaking day in and day out?

That is because,

1. You are not in the present moment.

The subconscious mind is running almost 90% of your life. Ever noticed when you are driving to the movies, but instinctively you begin taking the way to your office where you go every day, and then realise you are going the wrong way and correct your course? This proves that we are not in the present moment most of the time, but our subconscious mind, the perfect servant, is driving our lives. So, most of the time, you are not present (consciously) when you are doing affirmations.

2. The conscious mind is not in the record mode

For most adults, the beta brain waves are active. But when the brain is in alpha or theta waves, this is when it is learning and recording information. Children up to the age of 7 years are primarily in this brain wave stage. When you are in a hypnotic state or deep meditation, your brain wave is in alpha or theta. This means that when you are doing affirmations, you are yelling at a record player to record and play what you want. No matter how much you yell or plead, it is only when the record button is switched on that the new information will be processed and learned.

3. Mind is in the survival mode

The brain can exist in either of the two modes — Growth or Survival. We live in stressful times, and being overwhelmed and stressed triggers the brain to run in survival mode. This means the brain is so occupied with making sure you get through life that it is not learning anything new. The survival brain is too focused on keeping you alive. This could be triggered because of chronic stress, trauma or PTSD. So, until the body, mind, and, more specifically, the nervous system doesn't feel safe and soothed, the affirmations will not enter the mind to turn into behaviours.

4. Old beliefs come in the way

Usually, the affirmations are about being abundant, rich, having a partner or a happy relationship, health, peace, etc. But you also have certain beliefs and patterns running in the background in your subconscious mind, which are in direct contrast to the affirmations you are making to make your life better in some aspect. When you say the affirmation, let's say, "I am capable of earning XYZ amount of money", the subconscious mind says, "Yeah, right! You are not good enough to earn that". The belief "I am not good enough" interferes with the new thought, and the mind will always reject something new that is not in line with what you truly believe.

How to effectively use Affirmations to deal with emotions and moods

You now know that emotions happen because of how you process the information from the world (your thoughts and perceptions). Affirmations can be a useful way to help you develop a better thought process and perspective.

Here are a few ways to help you work with affirmations more successfully.

1. Affirmations with awareness

The first block to affirmations not working is the inability to always be in the present moment. As long as you are not healed from the past (traumas and insecurities), chances are you will either keep reliving it and stay in the past memories or be worrying about it or daydreaming about a different set of circumstances in the future.

Both these scenarios happen because either the present moment is not good enough or interesting enough as per your expectation. There is a lack of interest in the present moment, the NOW, because you are bored or you feel emotional pain, frustration, and overwhelmed to deal with the problems in the present situation. This creates the need to escape it somehow.

If you want the affirmations to work, you want to start doing them when you are more conscious and aware. You want to feel the words and the energy behind the words for the affirmations to begin to work. Keep doing it enough number of times, and you will find that at some moments, it feels natural when you speak those affirming words and statements. So, speak with complete consciousness in the moment.

A good practice to build awareness:

Every hour, bring your attention to your third eye (between your eyebrows) and answer these three questions:

1. What am I feeling right now?
2. What am I thinking right now?
3. What am I doing right now?

2. Practice meditation before affirmations

The next block you encounter is that the mind is not always in record mode. It is just playing back all your old programs and running the same tunes of old beliefs and patterns. The only time when your mind will learn and absorb new information is in a hypnotic state or in deep meditation.

I have described different methods of meditation in this book previously. You can use one of those techniques to begin to build your practice. You can also connect with a trained hypnotherapy professional or learn hypnosis for yourself to reach hypnotic states. Any affirmations done during or immediately after hypnosis or meditation will be effective.

Here is a meditation process to begin with using affirmations. This meditation is simple and only takes 5 - 15 minutes each day.

1. Find a comfortable position for meditation, whether it's sitting in the lotus posture or simply in a chair with your back straight. Take a moment to let go of any worries or tensions, allowing your body and mind to fully relax. Close your eyes gently to begin your practice.
2. Bring your hands together in a prayer position, positioned in front of your heart chakra. Allow a slight gap between your hands to sense the energy flowing between them.

3. Inhale deeply through your nose, drawing in positive energy.
4. Direct your focus to the empty space between your palms, shifting your consciousness to that space.
5. If thoughts arise, observe them without attachment, allowing them to pass, and gently bring your attention back to the space between your palms.
6. After a few moments, repeat your chosen affirmation while remaining in a meditative state. Speak the affirmation consciously and with awareness, working with one affirmation at a time.
7. When you feel complete, take three deep breaths, expressing gratitude to the positive energy for manifesting the affirmation's truth. Slowly open your eyes, returning to the present moment.

Do this for 5 to 15 minutes each day. You can do this at the beginning of the day, as an end-of-the-day process or at any time of the day when you want to feel centred and do your affirmations.

3. Do your inner work

Your limiting beliefs or patterns act as brakes when you are trying to accelerate your progress with affirmations. This is like driving a carriage with horses on opposite sides pulling the carriage in different directions; there can be no progress in this manner.

Some examples of limiting beliefs when working with affirmations are

Affirmation	Limiting Belief/Negative thought pattern
I can write a book that will add value to everyone who reads it	Nobody will read my book because no one cares what I have to say
I am worthy of what I desire.	I don't deserve anything good because I am not good enough
Money comes easily to me.	Money is evil. It makes people arrogant and bad.
I can achieve what I set my mind to	I am not talented enough. I am too young/old/inexperienced
I deserve a loving relationship	They will cheat on me Why would someone love me? I am not loveable
I accomplish my goals with ease	I won't get it right Something will go wrong
I prioritise my well-being I am important too	It's wrong to prioritise myself What will they say They won't talk to me if I ignore them

As long as the limiting beliefs or negative thought patterns keep being true for you, it will be almost impossible for any affirmations to work that go against that thought.

This is where inner work is needed to understand and change all those beliefs and patterns that prevent you from being happy and successful. Inner work means unravelling the "WHY" behind your behaviour —

- Why do I feel this way?
- Why do I behave this way?
- Why am I unable to get what I so desperately want?

Most of the time, the reasons are that you learned specific beliefs or patterns in your childhood through your own experiences, decisions made in certain situations, or by observing people's behaviour around you, and those learnings are a part of your belief system.

One way of understanding belief systems or patterns is this — beliefs are the rules by which we live our lives and create and attract experiences. They are written subconsciously through intense emotional experiences — positive or negative.

When we observe those events, let go of emotions felt in those moments and process what happened; we are able to look at what really happened objectively and learn or make better decisions or beliefs.

This is where therapy in the form of EFT, NLP and hypnosis helps. All these tools help you access the subconscious mind to rewrite the rules that are healthier and supportive for you so that your affirmations can work and you can manifest what you desire.

4. Connect to the feelings of success (fake it till you make it)

Picture this:

You are affirming every day to manifest more money or opportunities. You are writing the affirmations, chanting them and doing everything that is supposed to be done.

But when you are speaking the affirmations, you are not really believing that it can happen for you. You still feel doubtful or still work from a scarcity mindset. When an opportunity arises, your mind constantly doubts if you will get it, if you can handle it, if you deserve it. And the affirmations don't end up working, neither do the opportunities.

Looks familiar?

Affirmations work just like the Law of Attraction; you want to use them from a space of what you want to manifest. It means if you are manifesting money, you want to feel the feelings of already having money when affirming; if you are manifesting love, you want to believe that you already have love; if you are affirming for good health, you need to be able to visualise what good health looks like and what it feels like to be healthy.

Fake it till you make it. Remember the lemon experiment in mind-body connection — what your body feels, the mind thinks, and what your mind thinks, your body feels. You cannot manifest or make an affirmation work until you believe what you are doing will work or until you are not connected to the vibrational plane of what you want to manifest. You have to fake the feeling of already having what you want in order for your affirmations to work and help you manifest the result[23].

For example, if you want to manifest money, close your eyes and visualise the feeling of having money, notice where you see it in your life, what are you doing with it, how you feel having your desired amount of money, what is the feeling while receiving it, saving it and spending it. You want to have a feel of the experience of having money.

Once you have visualised and felt the feeling, notice which part of the visualisation was difficult, when your subconscious mind began to protest or oppose, and what thoughts came up that were doubtful or contrary to achieving what you want. These are your limiting beliefs or areas of self-sabotage. This is an area where you need to do the inner work.

Making affirmations work is about raising your vibrations to the plane of what you want. Sometimes, faking the feeling helps you tune into that vibration[24].

5. Practice Gratitude

Gratitude is a powerful way to connect to the energies of what you want. It indicates to the universe that you have already received what you wanted.

Gratitude is an instant way to connect you to the new vibrational plane. When you are grateful for something, you acknowledge having the gift and love it. This relaxes the body subliminally and sends a message to your brain that all is well in the world. It goes a long way in releasing the stress from the body.

Since stress keeps you in survival mode where growth cannot happen, when the body begins to release the stress, this raises its vibrations automatically.

Gratitude is a way of acknowledging what you have. And when you do that, the universe sends you more of it. Gratitude is a powerfully positive emotion; when you are grateful, you respond with Kindness, love and generosity. When you follow affirmations with gratitude, it amplifies their effect.

Some Examples of such affirmations are:

"I am worthy of all the good things. Thank you."

"I have a loving relationship that nurtures me. Thank you."

Gratefulness is like a muscle that can be developed. If you have never tried this consciously, do it right now. Observe around you all the things, and notice one good thing that happened today. Take a deep breath and, with eyes closed, speak out these words:

"*Thank you for* _____"

Gratitude can be a prayer, and it is the best form of prayer. It tells the universe or God that you appreciate what you have and you are going to nurture and cherish it. This creates feel-good hormones in the body - serotonin and dopamine. It makes you happy, uplifts your mood and attracts more such situations and things for which you can be grateful. It's a gift that keeps on giving.

> "*Gratitude blocks toxic emotions, such as envy, resentment, regret, and depression, which can destroy our happiness.*
> *— Robert Emmons, Professor at UC Davis*"

Putting it all together

Pick up your gratitude journal — a diary where you can write your affirmations with gratefulness. This is like your constant companion in your journey of emotional healing.

The best way to frame affirmations is to word them in the present tense and write them as if what you want has already happened.

Some examples of good affirmations for emotional balance and health:

- "I am grateful."
- "I recover from unsettling emotions, thank you."
- "I am proud of myself, thank you."
- "My feelings matter."
- "I forgive myself."
- "I am healing from this, thank you."
- "I acknowledge my emotion."
- "My life is abundant, thank you."

- "I am enough."
- "There isn't any need to doubt myself; what other people say doesn't matter. I'm the only person who can make me mad or keep me calm"

Speak your affirmations with awareness. Let each part of your body know that you are speaking magical words.

When you say any affirmation, do these two things:

1. Notice what you feel in the body and what your subconscious mind says (that critical voice inside the head) when you speak this affirmation. This is your area of inner work.
2. Connect to the feeling that you feel (or might feel) when you are not in the scarcity mindset.

CHAPTER NINETEEN

SPIRITUALITY

"We are not human beings having a spiritual experience. We are spiritual beings having a human experience."
— Pierre Teilhard de Chardin

Spirituality is a term that is often confused with meditation, rituals or a path. But if you look closely at the word, spirituality contains the word "spirit". Spirituality comes from the Latin word "spiritus", meaning "breath" of life.

Spirituality is not just a way of life. It is more than that. It is an attitude, a perspective through which you see the world. It is about acknowledging that in the grand scheme of things, I am but a minuscule speck.

Science today tells us that when we see the world, we do not always see reality; we see a version of the world that depends on how we perceive it based on our beliefs, thoughts, patterns, and values. All these factors were conditioned and learned in our childhood based on experiences and observations. This means that the situations we perceive as sad may not necessarily be as sad or may evoke another emotional response if our perception changes.

Indian spirituality, specifically the advaita philosophy, propounded this theory thousands of years ago that what we see in the world is just an illusion (Maya). The reality may be completely different.

If our life is like a beautiful tapestry, we live under the tapestry where we only see the knots and chaos of the threads. Rarely can we see above the chaos and behold the beautiful design of our life.

This is the essence of spirituality — we think what we see is the truth, but there is a bigger truth that we cannot see yet. It becomes the quest for many seekers — the quest of the ultimate truth of reality, or nirvana. And this brings in the need and the desire to connect with something greater than ourselves, to show us the path and guide us on the journey. This could be a connection to God, someone in divine form or a Guru in human form who has travelled further than we have and is capable of guiding us ahead.

Difference between Spirituality and Religion

Spirituality is different from religion. Religion is usually about personal beliefs and practices. Spirituality is about seeking the ultimate truth of reality. One way to distinguish between religion and spirituality is — if you believe, you are religious; if you seek truth, you are spiritual.

A religious person closes their eyes and believes what they see is the truth. A spiritual person opens their eyes and seeks the truth of reality.

Religion is necessary; it provides an anchor in the external world, a point of steadiness, certainty, and faith to help you go within yourself. But it is an initial step. Its job is to help you go deeper within to seek your own truth, to seek THE truth (this is spirituality). Ramakrishna Paramhansa's story serves as a powerful reminder of this fact.

> *"Ramkrishna Paramhansa was a devotee of Maa Kali. Whenever He had visions of Kali, he would be filled with ecstasy. The Goddess Kali was a living entity for him; She danced in front of him, ate from his own hands, and came when he called. For Ramakrishna, Kali was his mother. But though his body and mind were filled with ecstasy, his being was aware that this ecstasy was a bondage, too.*
>
> *Totapuri was a wandering monk who only believed in the formless Brahman. When he met Ramakrishna, Totapuri realised his potential and initiated him into sanyas as he wanted Ramakrishna to take the ultimate step that would lead to formless meditation and enlightenment. However, Ramakrishna's devotion to Goddess Kali was so profound that nothing Totapuri said swayed him. He was stuck on his devotion.*
>
> *Finally, the monk told him, "You are empowering your emotion and your body; you are not empowering your awareness." Convinced, Ramakrishna agreed to empower his awareness. Yet whenever he would close his eyes, Maa Kali would dance in front of him, and he would be filled with ecstasy again.*
>
> *So Totapuri said, "The next time Kali appears, you have to take a sword and cut her into pieces." Ramakrishna asked, "Where do I get the sword from?"*

Totapuri replied, "From the same place you get Kali from. If you can create a whole Kali, why can't you create a sword? You can do it. If you are able to create a goddess, why can't you create a sword to cut her? Get ready."

Under the monk's guidance, he conjured up a sword in the same way that he conjured Maa Kali and cut ties with her. It was not easy for Ramakrishna to do it; with Maa Kali gone, he saw himself left alone without his mother. When Maa Kali dissolved, Ramakrishna merged with the formless concept. He stayed in silence for six whole days. When he opened his eyes, he became enlightened!"

It is when we seek within what we have been seeking outside, is when we realise the truth.

When one begins to walk on the path of spirituality (not religion), different levels of awareness open up with growth. Each level brings us closer to the truth and closer to Ananda. Ananda is literally translated to bliss, but it is not even bliss; it is a state of ease.

Spirituality and the Journey of Emotional Healing

Initiation into spirituality usually begins with an existential crisis, and the focus comes on finding a sense of purpose and meaning in life. Going through repeated cycles of emotional upheavals, adversity or unhappiness, a question arises: "Why me? Why am I going through this?"

It is extremely difficult to find answers to such questions when one is in the middle of an emotional storm.

As the frustration builds, the intensity of the questions increases until one begins to question the futility of it all. This is when the search for purpose begins with the question, "Why am I going through this?"

The answers still don't come; they rarely do at this point. But this is when a choice arises, albeit a difficult one — to continue asking these questions or to accept what happened. If one continues to be frustrated and keeps asking the same questions, the situation continues.

But if one chooses to accept whatever happened, a new question arises, "What do I do now?" "What next?" This is when one begins to pick up the pieces of life and put them back together in a different manner, ready to see what the new picture is. This is when one has let go of perfect pictures, of how it's supposed to be, the illusion of control. This is when one begins to understand surrender.

> "*Surrender does not mean inaction. It means letting go of the need to control the result. True surrender is when one accepts the situation and surrenders the results to the Universe or a God.*"

Surrender does not mean inaction. It means letting go of the need to control the result. True surrender is when one accepts the situation and surrenders the results to the Universe or a God.

But the surrender is still not total. A new version of control comes into being born out of uncertainty. As the new picture begins to set in, the effort to make it better and make it perfect begins. And the cycle begins again — building something new, controlling the process and outcome, things going out of control, chaos and uncertainty, frustration — coming back to the same question, "Why me again? Why am I going through this? Is it my karma, or is it part of a grand scheme?"

Again, the question, again, the choice; at each stage, the wisdom of surrender keeps deepening until one day, you understand the real meaning of surrender and choose differently. The questions begin to drop one by one. Each time, it might feel like you are back to square one, but it's not so; you are evolving still; you are at a similar place but on a different plane of awareness. When you learn to surrender, you break free from these cycles and enter another cycle.

It continues as you learn the meaning of surrender in different situations and ways.

Meaning of Surrender according to Bhagvada Gita

Bhagvada Gita talks about many forms of surrender. One of them is this:

"कर्मण्येवाधिकारस्ते मा फलेषु कदाचन |
मा कर्मफलहेतुर्भूर्मा ते सङ्गोऽस्त्वकर्मणि || 47 ||"

"Karmanye vadhikaraste Ma Phaleshu Kadachana,
Ma Karmaphalaheturbhurma Te
Sangostvakarmani"

"You have a right to perform your prescribed duties, but you are not entitled to the fruits of your actions.
Never consider yourself to be the cause of the results of your activities, nor be attached to

inaction."

Perform your duty without fixating on the outcomes it may yield. Results are not solely contingent upon our endeavours. Numerous factors influence outcomes, including our efforts, destiny (shaped by our past actions), divine will, the actions of others, collective karmic influences, environmental circumstances, and chance occurrences. By fretting over results, we invite anxiety when they differ from our desires or expectations.

Lord Krishna advises Arjun to give up concern for the results and instead focus solely on doing his duty and a good job. This is an aspect of Karma Yog. A Karma Yogi does his work with no selfish motive, as a duty with no attachment to results. Non-attachment is difficult; this is why Krishna suggests the path of surrender through Karma Yog.

When this surrender sets in, a sense of non-attachment begins to develop.

Truth about Non-attachment

Non-attachment is a highly misunderstood concept. It does not mean being a cold-hearted person who doesn't feel. On the contrary, a non-attached person feels everything; they are intensely compassionate. They are also aware of the truth of reality:

- What is happening is not in my control,
- Nothing is permanent in this universe, It is just a phase, and this too shall pass just like everything else,
- What is happening to anyone is a result of their actions or karma (past deeds),

- My feelings are an energy,
- The emotions are a response to the environment which makes me human,

A non-attached person is a compassionate person. Someone who is attached cannot be compassionate because compassion requires the ability to allow the other person to feel — pleasure or pain; they know it is a part of growth and evolution, the ultimate goal. A non-attached person is, therefore, better able to help guide someone through their pain and suffering without being sucked into it.

The Journey of Emotional Healing continues...

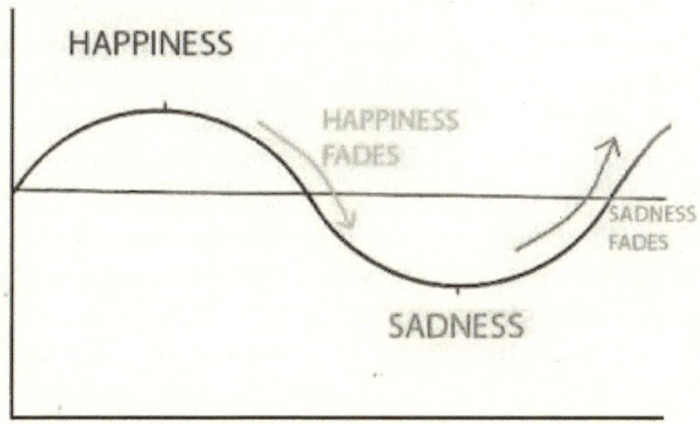

Therefore, when the illusion of control drops, non-attachment arises. It is non-attachment that helps you go through the cycles of joy and sadness with ease. As long as one is in the human body, emotions will be a truth.

Emotions have their own highs and lows. The problem arises when one gets attached to the highs and doesn't want them to go. But it's a cycle, and the wheel of fortune will always turn. This brings fear, uncertainty and insecurity of going into the lows. Therefore, when the lows arrive, the sadness and fear are extreme.

Extreme emotions wreak havoc on the mind and body. They cause all kinds of problems. One will want to run away from them because attachment is to happiness. And the wheel turns again, and the cycle shifts; because happiness was so eagerly coveted, it brings an intensity of feelings with it that intensifies the attachment. This enhances the fear of losing it, creating more anxiety, and the cycle continues of the downward spiral of mental, emotional and physical health.

At the same time, a non-attached person will be happy when the wheel of fortune favours him. But when the wheel turns, he will be sad too. There is neither attachment to happiness nor fear of sadness or struggle. As in the case of someone who is attached to happiness and ends up going in a downward spiral, the non-attached person moves into an equilibrium with time. The cycles are no longer extreme for them; the turn of the wheel affects less and less with time and practice.

When one is no longer on the emotional roller coaster, one becomes free to focus on one's purpose — whether it's service, seeking the truth or moksha.

Letting Go of the emotions held in the body

"I am not angry/sad/fear."
"I have feelings of anger/sadness/fear"

A non-attached person has the awareness of the separation of mind, body and soul. This separation provides objectivity. You are no longer defined by what you feel; you don't become the emotion. You just feel it as an energy arising. This helps you become capable of letting go of what you feel.

Letting go doesn't mean suppressing or forgetting it in a cupboard. It means really allowing the emotion and energy to leave the body because of the awareness that it is not you and it is a response of the body and mind to the environment.

Emotional Pain from Expectations

Expectations are considered natural in a relationship between individuals but also create emotional pain. Expectations are a result of attachment. Attachment is born out of fear.

> " *"I will be in pain if that person is not in my life."* "

It's not love, its fear of loss or abandonment. This creates attachment, expectations and subsequent pain.

As long as the other person exists to fill a gap inside you, you are not free. Bondage is another name for attachment. If you are full of love, overflowing with love, you don't need anyone to give you love or fill a gap inside you. Non-attachment fosters love. You can love only when you are not bound – when you are free.

When you don't need someone, you are truly free to connect with another being. Then, the question of being attached to someone doesn't even arise because there is no fear or a question of survival because of the loss of someone. Awareness takes the place of expectations.

Relationships created from non-attachment and true love are the healthiest of all. They provide room to grow, are nurturing and create happiness for all.

Illusion of Control

> "*The more you resist, the more it persists.*"

When you understand that control is an illusion and the fact that you cannot control anything in life except for how you think and behave, it sets you free from a lot of emotional upheaval and anxiety. Surrender to the Divine teaches you the futility of control. Need for Control is at the heart of most emotional issues and anxiety. At its core is fear.

Control is a form of resistance to the flow of life because of fear of life. And when you resist something, it will persist harder. So often, we are the ones standing in our own way to happiness. All we need is to get out of our way and let life happen.

Let go of the control to let the Universe do its job. Surrender to the Divine, trust in the unfolding of life and embrace the present moment. It will transform you.

When you have done your inner work, evolved your thought process and enhanced your awareness of the reality of ultimate truth, the need for control drops, and surrender becomes a way of life.

Essentially, your journey of emotional healing becomes an instrument for your journey of spiritual awakening.

References

1. Detecting emotions with wireless signals https://news.mit.edu/2016/detecting-emotions-with-wireless-signals-0920

2. Šimić G, Tkalčić M, Vukić V, Mulc D, Španić E, Šagud M, Olucha-Bordonau FE, Vukšić M, R Hof P. Understanding Emotions: Origins and Roles of the Amygdala. Biomolecules. 2021 May 31;11(6):823. doi: 10.3390/biom11060823. PMID: 34072960; PMCID: PMC8228195.

3. Gustafson C. Bruce Lipton, PhD: The Jump From Cell Culture to Consciousness. Integr Med (Encinitas). 2017 Dec;16(6):44-50. PMID: 30936816; PMCID: PMC6438088.

4. https://traumaticstress.nhs.wales/children-and-young-people/trauma-and-the-brain/#

5. Greenberg DM, Baron-Cohen S, Rosenberg N, Fonagy P, Rentfrow PJ. Elevated empathy in adults following childhood trauma. PLoS One. 2018 Oct 3;13(10):e0203886. doi: 10.1371/journal.pone.0203886. PMID: 30281628; PMCID: PMC6169872.

6. Watson, D., & Clark, L. A. (1994). Introduction to the special issue on personality and psychopathology. *Journal of Abnormal Psychology*, *103*(1), 3.

7. Nettle D, Bateson M. The evolutionary origins of mood and its disorders. Curr Biol. 2012 Sep 11;22(17):R712-21. doi: 10.1016/j.cub.2012.06.020. PMID: 22975002.

8. Broome MR, Saunders KE, Harrison PJ, Marwaha S. Mood instability: significance, definition and measurement. Br J Psychiatry. 2015 Oct;207(4):283-5. doi: 10.1192/bjp.bp.114.158543. PMID: 26429679; PMCID:

PMC4589661.

9. Power poses https://www.forbes.com/sites/kimelsesser/2018/04/03/power-posing-is-back-amy-cuddy-successfully-refutes-criticism/?sh=134c0d673b8e

10. Young SN. How to increase serotonin in the human brain without drugs. J Psychiatry Neurosci. 2007 Nov;32(6):394-9. PMID: 18043762; PMCID: PMC2077351.

11.https://www.healthdirect.gov.au/dopamine

12. Wudarczyk OA, Earp BD, Guastella A, Savulescu J. Could intranasal oxytocin be used to enhance relationships? Research imperatives, clinical policy, and ethical considerations. Curr Opin Psychiatry. 2013 Sep;26(5):474-484. doi: 10.1097/YCO.0b013e3283642e10. PMID: 23880593; PMCID: PMC3935449.

13. Pitkanen, M.. (2018). The experiments of Masaru Emoto with emotional imprinting of water. 10.13140/RG.2.2.24273.07524.

14. Travis FT, Wallace RK. Dosha brain-types: A neural model of individual differences. J Ayurveda Integr Med. 2015 Oct-Dec;6(4):280-5. doi: 10.4103/0975-9476.172385. PMID: 26834428; PMCID: PMC4719489.

15. Fresán U, Bes-Rastrollo M, Segovia-Siapco G, Sanchez-Villegas A, Lahortiga F, de la Rosa PA, Martínez-Gonzalez MA. Does the MIND diet decrease depression risk? A comparison with Mediterranean diet in the SUN cohort. Eur J Nutr. 2019 Apr;58(3):1271-1282. doi: 10.1007/s00394-018-1653-x. Epub 2018 Mar 7. PMID: 29516224.

16. Michal Kahn, Gal Sheppes, Avi Sadeh, Sleep and emotions: Bidirectional links and underlying mechanisms, International Journal of Psychophysiology, Volume 89, Issue 2, 2013, Pages 218-228, ISSN 0167-8760,

https://doi.org/10.1016/j.ijpsycho.2013.05.010.

17. Dinges, D. et al., Cumulative Sleepiness, Mood Disturbance, and Psychomotor Vigilance Decrements During a Week of Sleep Restricted to 4 – 5 Hours Per Night, Sleep. 1997 Apr; 20 (4): 267–277.

18. Ravaja, N., Harjunen, V., Ahmed, I. et al. Feeling Touched: Emotional Modulation of Somatosensory Potentials to Interpersonal Touch. Sci Rep 7, 40504 (2017).

19. Reiki and Healing Touch: Implications for Trauma Healing—Cynthia Ford, SIT Graduate Institute

20. S Teli S, Velou M S, L P, D D. An experimental Study on immediate effect of direct barefoot contact with earth on prehypertension. Int J Med Res Rev [Internet]. 2015Sep.30 [cited 2024Feb.8];3(8):836-40.

21. https://med.stanford.edu/news/all-news/2017/03/study-discovers-how-slow-breathing-induces-tranquility.html

22. Gerritsen R, et al. (2018). Breath of life: The respiratory vagal stimulation model of contemplative activity.https://www.ncbi.nlm.nih.gov/pmc/articles/PMC6189422/

23. Cascio, C.N. et al (2016). 'Self-Affirmation Activates Brain Systems associated with Self-Related Processing and Reward and is Reinforced by Future Orientation,' Social Cognitive and Affective Neuroscience, 11(4), 621-629

24.https://www.researchgate.net/publication/365211107_The_Power_of_the_Subconscious_Mind

25. The Quantum Mechanics of Changing Thoughts & the Frequency of Emotions. https://www.authenticityassociates.com/the-quantum-mechanics-of-changing-thoughts/

26. https://www.webmd.com/sleep-disorders/sleep-requirements

27. Sajjad, Z. B., Siddique, Y., Tariq, A., Suleman, Q., & Ashfaq, N. (2012). Study On Pattern Of Obsessive Behaviors And Thoughts In A State Of Anxiety In Teenagers. https://core.ac.uk/download/482118245.pdf

28. SCP-1280 - SCP Foundation. https://scp-wiki.wikidot.com/scp-1280

29. Ravaja, N., Harjunen, V., Ahmed, I., Jacucci, G., & Spapé, M. M. (2017). Feeling Touched: Emotional Modulation of Somatosensory Potentials to Interpersonal Touch. https://doi.org/10.1038/srep40504

30. How Touch Shapes Emotion | Greater Good. https://greatergood.berkeley.edu/article/item/how_touch_shapes_emotion

31. Dhyana or Meditation, the 7th limb of Ashtanga Yoga. https://www.shvasa.com/yoga-blog/what-is-dhyana-the-7th-limb-of-ashtanga-yoga

32. Good vibrations: How sound therapy aids wellbeing and emotional health - worldmedicinefoundation. https://worldmedicinefoundation.com/health-news/good-vibrations-how-sound-therapy-aids-wellbeing-and-emotional-health/

Recommended Books

The Bhagavad Gita

Discovering Psychology by **Hockenbury D. and Hockenbury SE.**

The Language of Emotions by **Karla McLaren**

Power vs Force by **Dr David Hawkins**

The Body Keeps the Score: Mind, Brain and Body in the Transformation of Trauma by **Bessel van der Kolk**

My Stroke of Insight by **Jill Bolte Taylor, PhD**

The Biology of Belief by **Dr Bruce Lipton**

The Science Behind Tapping by **Dr Peta Stapleton**

The Highly Sensitive Person **by Dr Elaine Aron**

You can Heal your Life by **Louise Hay**

The Book of Secrets by **Osho**

The Complete Works of Swami Vivekananda

About The Author

Meetu Sehgal is a Personal Transformation and Emotional Wellness Coach, EFT Trainer, Tarot Reader, Author, Intuitive Healer and Counselling Psychologist. With more than 15 years of experience in her field, she has been passionately working with individuals helping them resolve health, wealth and relationship challenges through coaching.

An intuitive healer, her journey into spirituality began very early with an introduction to the works of Swami Vivekananda, Bhagavad Gita and Osho. She brings this aspect of spirituality into her coaching and healing work, too, which sets it apart from the cut-and-dry tools of psychology.

She works with people from varied backgrounds, helping them heal their self-sabotaging patterns and emotional blocks to feel confident and empowered. She offers personal sessions, training, EFT, Inner Child Work (Matrix Re-imprinting), NLP, Tarot, Reiki and Angel Therapy.

Her workshops are interactive learning sessions, and coaching is a transforming experience. She conducts corporate and open-to-all workshops on emotional health (EFT) and well-being.

www.ingramcontent.com/pod-product-compliance
Lightning Source LLC
LaVergne TN
LVHW041026150826
845672LV00001B/217

* 9 7 9 8 8 9 2 7 7 4 4 0 6 *